How to Make a Florida Will

Seventh Edition

Mark Warda
Attorney at Law

SPHINX® PUBLISHING
AN IMPRINT OF SOURCEBOOKS, INC.®
NAPERVILLE, ILLINOIS
www.SphinxLegal.com

Seventh Edition, 2004

Published by: Sphinx® Publishing, A Division of Sourcebooks, Inc.®

Naperville Office
P.O. Box 4410
Naperville, Illinois 60567-4410
630-961-3900
Fax: 630-961-2168
www.sourcebooks.com
www.SphinxLegal.com

This publication is designed to provide accurate and authoritative information in regard to the subject matter covered. It is sold with the understanding that the publisher is not engaged in rendering legal, accounting, or other professional service. If legal advice or other expert assistance is required, the services of a competent professional person should be sought.

From a Declaration of Principles Jointly Adopted by a Committee of the American Bar Association and a Committee of Publishers and Associations

This product is not a substitute for legal advice.

Disclaimer required by Texas statutes.

Library of Congress Cataloging-in-Publication Date
Warda, Mark.
  How to make a Florida will / by Mark Warda.-- 7th ed.
    p. cm.
  Includes index.
  ISBN 1-57248-456-X (alk. paper)
  1. Wills--Florida--Popular works. I. Title.
KFF144.Z9W37 2004
346.75905'4--dc22
                          2004004774

Printed and bound in the United States of America.
VHG — 10 9 8 7 6 5 4 3 2 1

CONTENTS

USING SELF-HELP LAW BOOKS

Before using a self-help law book, you should realize the advantages and disadvantages of doing your own legal work and understand the challenges and diligence that this requires.

The Growing Trend

Rest assured that you won't be the first or only person handling your own legal matter. For example, in some states, more than seventy-five percent of the people in divorces and other cases represent themselves. Because of the high cost of legal services, this is a major trend and many courts are struggling to make it easier for people to represent themselves. However, some courts are not happy with people who do not use attorneys and refuse to help them in any way. For some, the attitude is, "Go to the law library and figure it out for yourself."

We write and publish self-help law books to give people an alternative to the often complicated and confusing legal books found in most law libraries. We have made the explanations of the law as simple and easy to understand as possible. Of course, unlike an attorney advising an individual client, we cannot cover every conceivable possibility.

Cost/Value
Analysis
Whenever you shop for a product or service, you are faced with various levels of quality and price. In deciding what product or service to buy, you make a cost/value analysis on the basis of your willingness to pay and the quality you desire.

When buying a car, you decide whether you want transportation, comfort, status, or sex appeal. Accordingly, you decide among such choices as a Neon, a Lincoln, a Rolls Royce, or a Porsche. Before making a decision, you usually weigh the merits of each option against the cost.

When you get a headache, you can take a pain reliever (such as aspirin) or visit a medical specialist for a neurological examination. Given this choice, most people, of course, take a pain reliever, since it costs only pennies; whereas a medical examination costs hundreds of dollars and takes a lot of time. This is usually a logical choice because it is rare to need anything more than a pain reliever for a headache. But in some cases, a headache may indicate a brain tumor and failing to see a specialist right away can result in complications. Should everyone with a headache go to a specialist? Of course not, but people treating their own illnesses must realize that they are betting on the basis of their cost/value analysis of the situation. They are taking the most logical option.

The same cost/value analysis must be made when deciding to do one's own legal work. Many legal situations are very straight forward, requiring a simple form and no complicated analysis. Anyone with a little intelligence and a book of instructions can handle the matter without outside help.

But there is always the chance that complications are involved that only an attorney would notice. To simplify the law into a book like this, several legal cases often must be condensed into a single sentence or paragraph. Otherwise, the book would be several hundred pages long and too complicated for most people. However, this simplification necessarily leaves out many details and nuances that would apply to special or unusual situations. Also, there are many ways to interpret most legal questions. Your case may come before a judge who disagrees with the analysis of our authors.

Therefore, in deciding to use a self-help law book and to do your own legal work, you must realize that you are making a cost/value analysis. You have decided that the money you will save in doing it yourself outweighs the chance that your case will not turn out to your satisfaction. Most people handling their own simple legal matters never have a problem, but occasionally people find that it ended up costing them more to have an attorney straighten out the situation than it would have if they had hired an attorney in the beginning. Keep this in mind while handling your case, and be sure to consult an attorney if you feel you might need further guidance.

Local Rules The next thing to remember is that a book which covers the law for the entire nation, or even for an entire state, cannot possibly include every procedural difference of every jurisdiction. Whenever possible, we provide the exact form needed; however, in some areas, each county, or even each judge, may require unique forms and procedures. In our state books, our forms usually cover the majority of counties in the state, or provide examples of the type of form which will be required. In our national books, our forms are sometimes even more general in nature but are designed to give a good idea of the type of form that will be needed in most locations. Nonetheless, keep in mind that your state, county, or judge may have a requirement, or use a form, that is not included in this book.

You should not necessarily expect to be able to get all of the information and resources you need solely from within the pages of this book. This book will serve as your guide, giving you specific information whenever possible and helping you to find out what else you will need to know. This is just like if you decided to build your own backyard deck. You might purchase a book on how to build decks. However, such a book would not include the building codes and permit requirements of every city, town, county, and township in the nation; nor would it include the lumber, nails, saws, hammers, and other materials and tools you would need to actually build the deck. You would use the book as your guide, and then do some work and research involving such matters as whether you need a permit of some kind, what type and grade of wood are available in your area, whether to use hand tools or power tools, and how to use those tools.

Before using the forms in a book like this, you should check with your court clerk to see if there are any local rules of which you should be aware, or local forms you will need to use. Often, such forms will require the same information as the forms in the book but are merely laid out differently or use slightly different language. They will sometimes require additional information.

Changes in the Law Besides being subject to local rules and practices, the law is subject to change at any time. The courts and the legislatures of all fifty states are constantly revising the laws. It is possible that while you are reading this book, some aspect of the law is being changed.

In most cases, the change will be of minimal significance. A form will be redesigned, additional information will be required, or a waiting period will be extended. As a result, you might need to revise a form, file an extra form, or wait out a longer time period; these types of changes will not usually affect the outcome of your case. On the other hand, sometimes a major part of the law is changed, the entire law in a particular area is rewritten, or a case that was the basis of a central legal point is overruled. In such instances, your entire ability to pursue your case may be impaired.

INTRODUCTION

This book was written to help Florida residents quickly and easily make their own wills without the expense or delay of hiring a lawyer. It begins with a short explanation of how a will works and what a will can and cannot do. It is designed to allow those with simple estates to quickly and inexpensively set up their affairs to distribute their property according to their wishes. It includes an explanation of how things such as *joint property* and *pay on death* accounts will affect your planning.

It also includes information on appointing a guardian for any minor children you may have. This can be useful in avoiding bad feelings between relatives and in protecting the children from being raised by someone you would object to.

Chapters 1 through 7 explain the laws that affect the making of a will. A glossary of terms is also included. Appendix A contains sample filled-in will forms to show you how it is done. Appendix B contains blank will forms you can use. A flow chart in Appendix B will help you choose the right will form based upon your circumstances and desires.

You can prepare your own will quickly and easily by using the forms out of the book, photocopying them, or retyping the material on sheets of paper. The small amount of time it takes to do this can give you and your loved ones the peace of mind of knowing that your estate will be distributed according to your wishes.

A surprising number of people have had their estates pass to the wrong parties because of a simple lack of knowledge of how the laws work. Before using any of the forms in Appendix B, you should read and understand all of the chapters of this book.

In each example given in the text you might ask, *What if my spouse dies first?* or *What if the children were grown up?* and then the answer might be different. If your situation is at all complicated, you are advised to seek the advice of an attorney. In many communities, wills are available for very reasonable prices. No book of this type can cover every contingency in every case, but a knowledge of the basics will help you to make the right decisions regarding your property.

The forms in this book are for simple wills to leave property to your family, or if you have no family, to friends or charities. As explained in Chapter 2, if you wish to disinherit your family and leave your property to others, consult with an attorney who can be sure that your will cannot be successfully challenged in court.

1 BASIC RULES YOU SHOULD KNOW

Before making your will, you should understand how a will works and what it can and cannot do. Otherwise, your plans may not be carried out and the wrong people may end up with your property. Understanding that a will is a document you can use to control who gets your property, who will be guardian of your children and their property, and who will manage your estate upon your death is the first step in properly creating and using a will. Understanding what a will is not and how to use your will is the focus of the rest of this chapter.

How a Will is Used

Some people think a will avoids *probate*—it does not. A *will* is the document used in probate to determine who receives the property and who is appointed guardian and executor or personal representative.

Avoiding Probate If you wish to avoid probate, you need to use methods other than a will, such as pay-on-death accounts, living trusts, or joint ownership. The first two of these are discussed later in this chapter. For information on living trusts, you should refer to a book that focuses on trusts as used for estate planning. (*The Living Trust Kit* by attorney Karen Ann Rolcik is available from the publisher of this book.)

If a person successfully avoids probate with all of his or her property, then he or she may not need a will. In most cases, when a husband or wife dies, no will or probate is necessary because everything is owned jointly. However, everyone should have a will in case property is accidentally not put into joint ownership, is received just prior to death and must go to probate, or if both husband and wife die in the same accident.

Joint Tenancy Avoids Probate

Property that is owned in *joint tenancy with right of survivorship* does not pass under a will. If a will gives property to one person, but it is already in a joint account with another person, the will is usually ignored and the joint owner of the account gets the property. This is because the property in the account avoids probate and passes directly to the joint owner. A will only controls property that goes through probate. There are exceptions to this rule. If money is put into a joint account only for convenience, it might pass under the will, but if the joint owner does not want to give it up, it could take an expensive court battle to get access to it.

Putting property into joint tenancy does not give the joint owner absolute rights to it. If the estate owes estate taxes, the recipient of joint tenancy property may have to contribute to the tax payment. Also, some states give spouses a right to property that is in joint accounts with other people. This is explained later in this chapter.

Example 1: Ted and his wife, Michelle, want all of their property to go to whoever survives the other. They put their house, cars, bank accounts, and brokerage accounts in joint ownership. When Ted dies, his wife only has to show his death certificate to get all of the property transferred to her name. No probate or will is necessary.

Example 2: After Ted's death, Michelle puts all of her property and accounts into joint ownership with her sons, Robert and Riley. Upon Michelle's death, her sons need only to present their mother's death certificate to have everything transferred into their names. No probate or will is necessary.

Joint Tenancy Overrules Your Will

If all property is in joint ownership or if all property is distributed through a will things are simple. But when some property passes by each method, a person's plans may not be fulfilled.

Example 1: Bill's will leaves all his property to his sister, Mary. Bill dies owning a house jointly with his wife, Joan, and a bank account jointly with his son, Don. Upon Bill's death, Joan gets the house, Don gets the bank account, and his sister, Mary, gets nothing.

Example 2: Betty's will leaves half her assets to Ann and half her assets to George. Betty dies owning $1,000,000 in stock jointly with George and a car in her name alone. Ann gets only a half interest in the car, while George gets all the stock and a half interest in the car.

Example 3: John's will leaves all his property equally to his five children. Before going in the hospital, he puts his oldest son, Harry, as a joint owner of his accounts. When John dies, Harry gets all of his assets. The rest of the children get nothing.

In each of these cases, the property went to a person it probably should not have because the decedent did not realize that joint ownership overruled his or her will. In some families, this might not be a problem. For example, Harry (from the third example) might divide the property equally (and possibly pay a gift tax) among his siblings. But in some cases, Harry would keep everything and the family would never talk to him again or would take him to court.

Joint Tenancy can be Risky

In many cases, joint property can be an ideal way to own property and avoid probate. However, it does have risks. If you put your real estate in joint ownership with someone, you cannot sell it or mortgage it without that person's signature. If you put your bank account in joint ownership with someone, they can take out all of your money.

Example 1: Alice put her house in joint ownership with her son. She later married Ed and moved in with him. She wanted to sell her house and to invest the money for income. Her son refused to sign the deed because he wanted to keep the home in the family. She was in court for ten months getting her house back and the judge almost refused to do it.

Example 2: Alex put his bank accounts into joint ownership with his daughter, Mary, to avoid probate. Mary fell in love with Doug, who was in trouble with the law. Doug talked Mary into *borrowing* $30,000 from the account for a *business deal* that went sour. Later she *borrowed* $25,000 more to pay Doug's bail bond. Alex did not find out until it was too late and his money was gone.

You can get the same benefits of joint tenancy without the risks by setting up your accounts through a *transfer of death* (TOD) method as explained on page 7.

Tenancy in Common does not Avoid Probate

In most states there are three basic ways to own property—joint tenancy with right of survivorship, tenancy in common, and an estate by the entireties. *Joint tenancy with right of survivorship* means if one owner of the property dies, the survivor automatically gets the decedent's share. *Tenancy in common* means when one owner dies, that owner's share of the property goes to his or her heirs or beneficiaries under the will. An *estate by the entireties* is like joint tenancy with right of survivorship, but it can only apply to a married couple and is only recognized in some states.

Example 1: Tom and Marcia bought a house together and lived together for twenty years but were never married. The deed did not specify joint tenancy. When Tom died, his bother inherited his half of the house, and it had to be sold because Marcia could not afford to buy it from him.

Example 2: Lindsay and her husband, Rocky, bought a house. When Rocky suddenly died, Lindsay obtained full ownership of the house by filing a death certificate at the courthouse. That was because the deed to the house stated that they were husband and wife, so ownership was presumed to be estate by the entireties.

When property is held in joint tenancy with right of survivorship or as an estate by the entireties it avoids probate, but property titled with tenancy in common does not.

A Spouse can Overrule a Will

Under Florida law a surviving spouse is entitled to thirty percent of a person's estate no matter what the person's will states. This is sometimes called the *elective share*. It is meant to protect a spouse from being left destitute.

Example 1: John's will leaves all his property to his children of a previous marriage and nothing to his second wife, who is already wealthy. The wife still gets thirty percent of John's estate, and his children divide the remaining seventy percent. (F.S. Sec. 732.201 *et seq.*)

> **NOTE:** *F.S. Sec. 732.201 et seq. is the citation for Florida Statutes Section 732.201 and following. This citation system will be used throughout the book.*

Example 2: Mary puts half of her property in a joint account with her husband, and in her will she leaves all of her other property to her sister. When she dies, her husband gets all the money in the joint account and thirty percent of all her other property.

If you do not plan to leave your spouse at least thirty percent of your estate, you should consult a lawyer.

A Spouse's Share can be Avoided

There are legitimate reasons to avoid giving a spouse the share allowed by law—such as when both spouses are wealthy or there are children from a previous marriage—and the law allows some exceptions.

The easiest way is for your spouse to sign a written agreement either before or after the marriage. While many spouses express the greatest fondness for their stepchildren, getting them to sign over a large share of an estate can be a challenge. When such an agreement is signed before marriage, it is called a *premarital agreement* or *antenuptial agreement* and when it is signed during the marriage it is called a *marital agreement.*

In the past, the easiest way to avoid the spouse's elective share was to put your property in trust or in joint tenancy with another person. For example, you could have your stocks in a joint account with your children and then your spouse would have no claim to them. The law now allows the spouse to have thirty percent of nearly all property owned by the deceased no matter how it was titled.

There are questions as to whether this law is constitutional and if so, if it is enforceable against property in another state. There is also an issue of how a spouse will even know about all property if, for example, there are out-of-state safe deposit boxes or accounts. However, if you try to avoid the spouse's share by putting your funds in another state with your children, it may cost your estate more in lawyer's fees to find out whether it was legal or not.

If you do not plan to leave your spouse at least thirty percent of your estate, you should enter into a marital agreement with your spouse to be sure that your plans will not be challenged after death. In this situation it would be best to consult with an estate planning attorney.

Avoiding a spouse's share, especially without his or her knowledge, opens the possibility of a lawsuit after your death. If your actions were not done to precise legal requirements, they could be thrown out. Therefore, you should consider consulting an attorney if you plan to leave your spouse less than the share provided by law.

TOD Bank Accounts are Better than Joint Ownership

One way to keep bank accounts out of probate and still retain control of them is to set them up as *transfer on death* (*TOD*) accounts with a named beneficiary. Some banks use the letters *POD* (*pay on death*) or *I/T/F* (*in trust for*). Either way, the result is the same. No one except you can get the money until your death, at which time it immediately goes directly to the person you name, without a will or probate proceeding. These are sometimes called *Totten Trusts* after the court case that declared them legal.

> ***Example:*** Rich opened a bank account in the name of "Rich, TOD Mary." When Rich dies, the money automatically goes to Mary, but prior to his death Mary has no control over the account. Mary does not even have to know about it, and Rich can take her name off the account at any time.

Securities Registered TOD

The drawback of the Totten Trust has been that it was only good for cash in a bank account. Stocks and bonds still had to go through probate. But Florida has adopted the *Uniform Transfer on Death Security Registration Act* allowing TOD accounts. These can include stocks, bonds, mutual funds, and other similar investments. Now an estate with cash and securities can pass on death with no need for court proceedings.

To set up your securities to transfer automatically on death, you need to have them correctly registered. If you use a brokerage account, the brokerage company should have a form for you to do this.

If your securities are registered in your own name or with your spouse, you need to reregister them in TOD format with the designation of your beneficiary. The following illustrations of how to do so are contained in Florida Statute Sec. 711.511.

Sole owner with sole beneficiary:
> *John S Brown TOD John S Brown Jr*

Multiple owners with sole beneficiary (John and Mary are joint tenants with right of survivorship and when they die, John, Jr., inherits the property):

John S Brown Mary B Brown JT TEN TOD John S Brown Jr

Multiple owners—substituted beneficiary (John and Mary are joint tenants with right of survivorship, and when they die John Jr. inherits the property; but if John predeceases them, then Peter inherits it):

John S Brown Mary B Brown JT TEN TOD
John S Brown Jr SUB BEN Peter Q Brown

Multiple owners—lineal descendants (John and Mary are joint tenants with right of survivorship, and when they die John, Jr., inherits the property; but if John predeceases them, John, Jr.'s lineal descendants inherit it):

John S Brown Mary B Brown JT TEN TOD John S Brown Jr LDPS

You cannot Will Your Homestead

There are two meanings for the word *homestead* in Florida. One is the tax exemption that you get from the property appraiser when you reside on a property. This has nothing to do with whether the property is homestead for estate purposes. A homestead for estate purposes is property that is the permanent residence of a legal resident of Florida who has a spouse or minor children and who owns the property in his or her name alone.

If your property is homestead your will has no control over it. Upon your death your homestead automatically passes as follows.

✪ If you have both a spouse and minor children, your spouse gets the right to live in the homestead for the rest of his or her life and your children get it upon your spouse's death.

✪ If you have a spouse and no minor children, your spouse gets the homestead, no matter what your will says.

✪ If you have minor children but no spouse, your children get the homestead in equal shares, no matter what your will says.

Exception   If you have a spouse and grown children, you can will the homestead to your spouse.

Whether or not a home is a homestead is a tricky legal question. It may depend on which spouse is providing the support or whether or not the property is also being used for business purposes. If you have a question of whether your property is a homestead for estate purposes, consult a lawyer who is experienced in estate planning.

Because homestead property can only be property that is in individual ownership, jointly held property and property in trust does not come under these rules. To avoid property becoming homestead property, it must be purchased in joint names or in trust. If it is already in an individual's name, it cannot be put in trust or in joint ownership without the spouse's signature.

It is possible to set up the title to your home in such a way that it will not be homestead and your spouse cannot claim an interest in it (for example, if you want it to go to your children by a previous marriage). However, this should be done by a lawyer who is familiar with the latest cases in this area. If it is done incorrectly, it may be thrown out by a court. In such a situation you should also consider a written agreement with your spouse regarding the home.

Putting a Homestead in Trust

A homestead passing to a spouse or to children does not need to go through a formal probate, but it still requires a lawyer to file a petition with the court and a judge to rule on it. You can put a homestead into trust to avoid this, but there are two important issues to be concerned with.

Tax Exemption   To be sure not to lose your homestead tax exemption, you will either need to use special language in your trust or to keep a life estate in your property before deeding it into trust. Check with an attorney or your tax assessor before deeding your property into a trust.

Protection from Creditors   If you put your homestead in trust to avoid probate, it will be more at risk if you have creditors. The homestead of a Florida resident cannot be taken by a creditor because it is protected in the constitution, but this protection can be lost if the homestead is put into trust.

If you have no risks and good insurance, this may not be a problem. But if you are in a high-risk occupation or expect to have large debts, check with an attorney before putting your homestead into trust. If you have put your homestead into trust and have a creditor pursuing you, it may be possible to take the homestead out of trust and still claim the protection. Again, you will need the advice of an experienced attorney.

Some Property may be Exempt from Your Will

If you have a spouse or minor children, then up to $10,000 in *household furniture, furnishings, and appliances* in your *usual place of abode*, all automobiles in your name that are regularly used by you or members of your family, prepaid college accounts, and teacher's benefits are exempt from your will. This is called *exempt property*. If you have a spouse, then your spouse gets this property. If you have no spouse, your children receive it. Additionally, a spouse or minor children may receive a *family allowance* of up to $18,000. (F.S. Sec. 732.403.)

Example: Donna dies with a will giving half of her property to her husband and half to her grown son from a previous marriage. Donna's property consists of a $5,000 automobile, $5,000 in furniture, and $20,000 in cash. Donna's husband may be able to get the car and the furniture as exempt property and $18,000 as a family allowance. Then he and the son would split the remaining $2,000.

To avoid having property declared exempt, it may be specifically given to someone in a will. If certain items are specifically given to certain persons, those items will not be considered part of the exempt property. If cash is kept in a joint or TOD bank account, it would go to the joint owner or beneficiary and not be used as the family allowance.

IRAs and Pension Plans

Any pension plans and retirement accounts that you own can be set up to pass to someone automatically upon your death. You do this by designating a beneficiary with the company that holds the account. The beneficiary of your account gets the account regardless of what your will says. If you want your retirement account to pass to someone under your will, make the beneficiary of your retirement account *my estate* or leave it blank.

Life Insurance

In most cases, your life insurance will have a person named as beneficiary to receive the payout upon your death. The beneficiary of your policy gets the account regardless of what your will says. If you want your insurance proceeds to pass to someone under your will, make the beneficiary of your policy *my estate*.

Getting Married Automatically Changes Your Will

If you get married after making your will and do not rewrite it after the wedding, your spouse gets a share of your estate as if you had no will, unless you have a prenuptial agreement, you made a provision for your spouse in the will, or you stated in the will that you intended not to mention your prospective spouse. (F.S. Sec. 732.301.)

Example: John made out his will leaving everything to his physically-challenged brother. When he married Joan, an heiress with plenty of money, he did not change his will because he still wanted his brother to get his estate. When he died, Joan received John's entire estate and John's brother did not receive anything.

Getting Divorced Automatically Changes Your Will

A judgment of divorce automatically changes your will to the effect that the former spouse is treated as if he or she predeceased the maker of the will. (F.S. Sec. 732.507(2).)

Having Children may Automatically Change Your Will

If you have a child after making your will and do not rewrite it, the child may receive a share of your estate as if there was no will. (F.S. Sec. 732.302.)

Example: Dave made a will leaving half of his estate to his sister and the other half to be shared by his three children. He later had another child and did not revise his will. Upon his death, his fourth child would get one quarter of his estate, his sister would get three-eighths, and the other three children would each get one-eighth.

It is best to rewrite your will at the birth of a child. However, another solution is to include this clause after the names of your children in your will:
  …and any afterborn children living at the time of my death, in equal shares.

If you have one or more children and are leaving all of your property to your spouse, then your will would not be affected by the birth of a subsequent child.

How Your Debts are Paid

One of the duties of the person administering an estate is to pay the debts of the decedent. Before an estate is distributed, the legitimate debts must be ascertained and paid.

An exception is *secured debts* (debts that are protected by a lien against property, like a home loan or a car loan). In the case of a secured debt, the loan does not have to be paid before the property is distributed.

Example: John owns a $100,000 house with a $80,000 mortgage, and he has $100,000 in the bank. If he leaves the house to his brother and the bank account to his sister, then his brother would receive the home but would owe the $80,000 mortgage.

What if your debts are more than your property? Today, unlike hundreds of years ago, people cannot inherit other peoples' debts. A person's property is used to pay his or her probate and funeral expenses first, and if there is not enough left to pay his or her other debts, then the creditors are out of luck. However, if a person leaves property to people and does not have enough assets to pay his or her debts, then the property will be sold to pay the debts.

Example: Jeb's will leaves all of his property to his three children. At the time of his death, Jeb, has $30,000 in medical bills, $11,000 in credit card debt, and his only assets are his car and $5,000 in stock. The car and stock would be sold and the funeral bill and probate fees paid out of the proceeds. If any money was left, it would go to the creditors and nothing would be left for the children. The children would not have to pay the medical bills or credit card debt.

Estate and Inheritance Taxes

Unlike some states, Florida does not have estate or inheritance taxes in most cases. The only time estate taxes would be paid to the state of Florida would be if the estate was subject to federal estate taxes and a credit was allowed for state taxes. Then these taxes would be paid to the state and credited against the federal tax due.

There is a federal estate tax for estates above a certain amount. Estates below that amount are allowed a *unified credit* that exempts them from tax. The unified credit applies to the estate a person can leave at death and to gifts during his or her lifetime. At present, the federal government only taxes estates at $1,500,000 and higher. This amount will rise to $3,500,000 by 2009. In 2010, the tax is scheduled for complete repeal, then in 2011, it comes back with the exemption back down to $1,000,000. The law will most likely change again before 2011, so you would be well advised to keep up with the changes.

The following chart shows how the exempt estates are scheduled to rise.

Year	Amount
2004–2005	$1,500,000
2006–2008	$2,000,000
2009	$3,500,000

Annual Exclusion

When a person makes a gift, that gift is subtracted from the amount entitled to the unified credit available to his or her estate at death. However, a person is allowed to make gifts of up to $11,000 per person per year without having these subtracted from the unified credit. This means a married couple can make gifts of up to $22,000 per person. The *Taxpayer Relief Act of 1997* provides that this exclusion amount be adjusted for inflation.

2 THE NEED FOR A FLORIDA WILL

Everyone needs to examine their own situation to determine if they need a will, what it can and cannot do for them, and what type of will will work best.

What a Will can Do

A will allows you to decide who gets your property after your death. This is generally the foremost reason people create a will. You can give specific personal items to certain persons and choose which of your friends or relatives, if any, deserve a greater share of your estate. You can also leave gifts to schools and charities. Some other very important reasons to create a will include the following.

Personal Representative

A will allows you to decide who will be in charge of handling your estate. This is the person who gathers together all your assets and distributes them to the beneficiaries, hires attorneys or accountants if necessary, and files any essential tax or probate forms. In Florida, this person is called the *personal representative*. (In other states he or she is called the *executor* or *executrix*.) With a will, you can provide that your personal representative does not have to post a surety bond with the court in order to serve and this can save your estate some money. You can also give him or her the power to sell your property and take other actions without getting a court order.

Guardian   A will allows you to choose a guardian for your minor children. This way you can avoid arguments among relatives and make sure the best person raises your children. You may also appoint separate guardians over your children and over their money. For example, you may appoint your sister as guardian over your children and your father as guardian over their money. That way, a second person can keep an eye on how the children's money is being spent.

You can set up a trust to provide that your property is not distributed immediately. Many people feel that their children would not be ready to handle large sums of money at the age of majority, which in most states is 18. A will can direct that the money is held until the children are 21, 25, or older.

If your estate is over the amount protected by the federal *unified credit* ($1,500,000 in 2004-2005, but will be rising to $3,500,000 by the year 2009), then it will be subject to federal estate taxes. If you wish to lower those taxes, for example by making gifts to charities, you can do so through a will. However, such estate planning is beyond the scope of this book and you should consult an estate planning attorney or another book for further information.

What not having a Will can Do

If you do not have a will, Florida law provides that your property shall be distributed as follows.

- ✪ If you leave a spouse and no children, your spouse gets your entire estate.

- ✪ If you leave a spouse and children who are all children of your spouse, then your spouse gets the first $60,000 and half of the balance. The children get equal shares of the remainder.

- ✪ If you leave a spouse and at least one child who is not your spouse's child, then your spouse gets half of your estate and all of your children get equal shares of the other half.

- ✪ If you leave no spouse, all of your children get equal shares of your estate.

✪ If you leave no spouse and no children, then your estate would go to the highest persons on the following list who are living:

- your parents;

- your brothers and sisters, or if dead, their children;

- your grandparents;

- your uncles and aunts or their descendants; or,

- relatives of your deceased spouse.

The Validity of Your Out-of-State Will in Florida

A will that is valid in another state would probably be valid to pass property in Florida. However, if the will is not *self-proved*, a person in your former state would have to be appointed as a *Commissioner* to take the oath of a person who witnessed your signature on the will before it could be accepted by a Florida Probate Court. Because of the expense and delay in having a Commissioner appointed and the problems in finding out-of-state witnesses, it is advisable to execute a new will after moving to Florida.

Florida also allows a will to be self-proved so that the witnesses never have to be called in to take an oath. With special self-proving language in your will, the witnesses take the oath at the time of signing and never have to be seen again.

Another advantage to having a Florida will is that as a Florida resident, your estate will pay no state probate or inheritance taxes. If you move to Florida but keep your old will, your former state of residence may try to collect taxes on your estate.

Example: George and Barbara left their high-tax state and retired to Florida, which has no estate or inheritance taxes, but they never made a new will. Upon their deaths, their former state of residence tried to collect a tax from their estate because their old wills stated that they were residents of that state.

What a Will cannot Do

A will cannot direct that anything illegal be done and it cannot put unreasonable conditions on a gift. A provision that your daughter gets all of your property if she divorces her husband would be ignored by the court. She would get the property with no conditions attached. You can put some conditions in your will. To be sure they are enforceable, consult with an attorney.

A will cannot leave money or property to an animal because animals cannot legally own property. If you wish to continue paying for care of an animal after your death, leave the funds in trust or to a friend whom you know will care for the animal.

Using a Simple Will

The wills in this book will pass your property whether your estate is $1,000 or $100,000,000. However, if your estate is over $1,500,000 (in 2004–2005, rising to $3,500,000 by 2009), then you might be able to avoid estate taxes by using a trust or other tax-saving device. The larger your estate, the more you can save on estate taxes by doing more complicated planning. If you have a large estate and are concerned about estate taxes, you should consult an estate planning attorney or a book on estate planning.

When a Simple Will should not be Used

There are times and situations when a simple will does not adequately achieve your goals. In those situations, it makes more sense to consult an attorney to ensure that your needs will be met. Some of these situations include the following.

- ✪ If you expect that there may be a fight over your estate or that someone might *contest* your will's validity, then you should consult a lawyer.

- ✪ If you leave less than the *statutory share* (30% of your estate) to your spouse. (see p.5.)

- ✪ If you leave one or more of your children out of your will.

- ✪ If you are the *beneficiary of a trust* or have any complications in your legal relationships, you may need special provisions in your will.

- ✪ A person who is *blind* or who can sign only with an "X" should also consult a lawyer about the proper way to make and execute a will.

- ✪ If you expect to have *over $1,500,000* (in 2004–2005, rising to over $3,500,000 by 2009) at the time of your death, you may want to consult with a CPA or tax attorney regarding tax consequences.

- ✪ If you wish to put some sort of *conditions* or restrictions on the property you leave. For example, if you want to leave money to your brother only if he quits smoking or to a hospital only if they name a wing in your honor, consult an attorney to be sure that your conditions are valid.

3 How to Make a Simple Will

Any person who is eighteen years of age and of sound mind can make a valid will in Florida. If you meet this basic requirement, you need to think about what to include in your will and how to properly prepare it.

Identifying Parties in Your Will

When making your will, it is important to clearly identify the persons you name as your beneficiaries. In some families, names differ only by middle initial or by Jr. or Sr. Be sure to check everyone's name before making your will. You can also add your relationship to the beneficiary and their location, such as *my cousin, George Simpson of Clearwater, Florida.*

The same applies to organizations and charities. For example, there is more than one group using the words *cancer society* or *heart association* in their name. Be sure to get the correct name of the group to which you intend to leave your gift.

Spouse and Children It is a good idea to mention your spouse and children in your will even if you do not leave them any property. That will show that you are of sound mind and know who are your heirs. As mentioned earlier, if you have a spouse and/or children and plan to leave your property to persons other than them, you should consult an attorney to be sure that your will will be enforceable.

Personal Property

Because people acquire and dispose of personal property so often, it is not advisable to list a lot of small items in your will. Otherwise, when you sell or replace one of them, you may have to rewrite your will.

One solution is to describe the type of item you wish to give. For example, instead of saying, *I leave my 2000 Ford to my sister*, you should say, *I leave any automobile I own at the time of my death to my sister.*

Of course, if you do mean to give a specific item, you should describe it. For example instead of *I leave my diamond ring to Joan*, you should say, *I leave to Joan the one-half carat diamond ring that I inherited from my grandmother*, because you might own more than one diamond ring at the time of your death.

Handwritten List of Personal Property In Florida, you are allowed to leave a handwritten list of personal items (other than money or property used in a trade or business) that you wish to go to certain people and this would be legally binding. (F.S. Sec. 732-515.) The wills in this book include a clause stating that you may leave such a list. This list must be signed by you. It may be made before or after your will, and it may be changed at any time. It does not need to be witnessed.

Specific Bequests

Occasionally, a person will want to leave a little something to a friend or charity and the rest to the family. This can be done with a *specific bequest* such as *$1,000 to my dear friend Martha Jones*. Of course, there could be a problem if, at the time of a person's death, there wasn't anything left after the specific bequests.

Example: At the time of making his will, Todd had $1,000,000 in assets. He felt generous, so he left $50,000 to a local hospital, $50,000 to a local group that took care of homeless animals, and the rest to his children. Unfortunately, several years later, the stock market crashed and he committed suicide. His estate at the time was worth only $110,000 so after the above specific bequests, the legal fees, and expenses of probate, there was nothing left for his five children.

Another problem with specific bequests is that some of the property may be worth considerably more or less at death than when the will was made.

Example: Joe wanted his two children to equally share his estate. His will left his son his stocks (worth $500,000 at the time) and his daughter $500,000 in cash. By the time of Joe's death the stock was only worth $100,000. He should have left *fifty percent* of his estate to each child.

If giving certain things to certain people is an important part of your estate plan, you can give specific items to specific persons, but remember to make changes if your assets change.

Joint Beneficiaries Be careful about leaving one item of personal property to more than one person. For example, if you leave something to your son and his wife, what would happen if they divorce? Even if you leave something to two of your own children, what if they cannot agree about who will have possession of it? Whenever possible, leave property to one person.

Remainder Clause

One of the most important clauses in a will is the *remainder clause*. This is the clause that says *all the rest of my property I leave to....* This clause makes sure that the will disposes of all property owned at the time of death and that nothing is forgotten.

In a simple will the best way to distribute property is to put it all in the remainder clause. In the first example in the previous section, the problem would have been avoided if the will had read as follows.

The rest, residue, and remainder of my estate I leave, five percent to ABC Hospital, five percent to XYZ Animal Welfare League, and ninety percent to be divided equally among my children.

Alternate Beneficiaries

Always provide for an *alternate beneficiary* in case the person you name dies before you and you do not have a chance to make out a new will.

Survivor or Descendants

Suppose your will leaves your property to your sister and brother, but your brother predeceases you. Should his share go to your sister or to your brother's children or grandchildren?

If you are giving property to two or more persons and if you want it all to go to the other if one of them dies, then you would specify *or the survivor of them.*

If, on the other hand, you want the property to go to the children of the deceased person, you should state *or their lineal descendants* in your will. This would include his or her children and grandchildren.

Family or Person

If you decide you want the property to go to your brother's children and grandchildren, you must next decide if an equal share should go to each family or to each person. For example, if your brother leaves three grandchildren, and one is an only child of his daughter and the others are the children of his son, should all grandchildren get equal shares, or should they take their parent's share?

When you want each family to get an equal share, it is called *per stirpes*. When you want each person to get an equal share, it is called *per capita*. Most of the wills in this book use per stirpes because that is the most common way property is left. If you wish to leave your property per capita, then you can rewrite the will with this change.

Example: Alice leaves her property to her two daughters, *Mary and Pat in equal shares, or to their lineal descendants per stirpes.* Both daughters die before Alice. Mary leaves one child; Pat leaves two children. In this case, Mary's child would get half of the estate and Pat's children would split the other half of the estate. If Alice had specified per capita instead of per stirpes then each child would have gotten one-third of the estate.

Per Stirpes Distribution

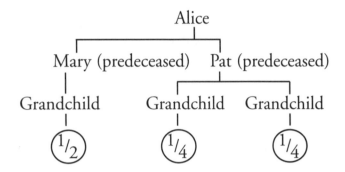

Per Capita Distribution

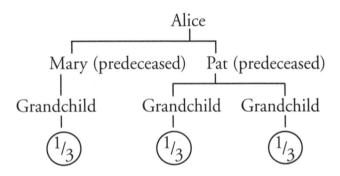

There are fourteen different will forms in this book that should cover the options most people want, but you may want to divide your property slightly differently from what is stated in these forms. If so, you can retype the forms according to these rules, specifying whether the property should go to the survivor or the lineal descendants. If this is confusing to you, you should consider seeking the advice of an attorney.

Survivorship

Many people put a clause in their will stating that anyone receiving property under the will must survive for thirty days (or forty-five or sixty) after the death of the person who made the will. This is so that if the two people die in the same accident, there will not be two probates and the property will not go to the other party's heirs.

Example: Fred and Wilma were married and each had children by previous marriages. They didn't have survivorship clauses in their wills and they were in an airplane crash and died. Fred's children hired several expert witnesses and a large law firm to prove that at the time of the crash, Fred lived for a few minutes longer than Wilma. That way, when Wilma died first, all of her property went to Fred. When he died a few minutes later, all of Fred and Wilma's property went to his children. Wilma's children got nothing.

Guardians

If you have minor children, you should name a guardian for them. There are two types of guardians—a guardian over the *person* and a guardian over the *property*. The first is the person who decides where the children will live and makes the other parental decisions for them. A guardian of the property is in charge of the minor's property and inheritance. In most cases, one person is appointed guardian of both the person and property. But some people prefer the children to live with one person, but to have the money held by another person.

Example: Sandra was a widow with a young daughter. She knew that if anything happened to her, her sister would be the best person to raise her daughter. But her sister was never good with money. So when Sandra made out her will, she named her sister as guardian over the person of her daughter and she named her father as guardian over the estate of her daughter.

When naming a guardian, it is always advisable to name an alternate guardian in case your first choice is unable to serve for any reason.

Children's Trust

When a parent dies leaving a minor child and the child's property is held by a guardian, the guardianship ends when the child reaches the age of eighteen. All the property is then turned over to the child. Most parents do not feel their children are competent at the age of eighteen to handle large sums of money and prefer that it be held until the child is 21, 25, 30, or even older.

If you wish to set up a complicated system of determining when your children should receive various amounts of your estate or if you want the property held to a higher age than 35, you should consult a lawyer to draft a trust. However, if you want a simple provision that the funds be held until they reach a higher age than 18 and you have someone you trust to make decisions about paying for education or other expenses for your child or children, you can put that provision in your will as a children's trust.

The children's trust trustee can be the same person as the guardian or a different person. It is advisable to name an alternate trustee if your first choice is unable to handle the funds.

Personal Representative

A *personal representative* is the person who will be in charge of your probate. He or she will gather your assets, handle the sale of them if necessary, prepare an inventory, hire an attorney, and distribute the property. This should be a person you trust, and if it is, then you can state in your will that no bond will be required to be posted by him or her. Otherwise, the court will require that a surety bond be paid for by your estate to guarantee that the person is honest. You can appoint a bank to handle your estate, but their fees are usually very high.

It is best to appoint a *resident* of your state, both because it is easier and because a bond may be required of a *non-resident* even if your will waives it.

Some people like to name two persons to handle their estate to avoid jealousy or to have them check on each other's honesty. However, this is not a good idea. It makes double work in getting the papers signed and there can be problems if they cannot agree on something.

The person handling your estate is entitled to compensation. (F.S. Sec. 733.613.) The fee is specified at three percent of the first million dollars of the estate but is lower for higher amounts. A family member will often waive the fee, but if there is a lot of work involved he or she may request the fee or other family members may insist that he or she take one. You can insist in your will that your personal representative is paid a fee.

In Florida, a personal representative cannot sell real estate without approval by the court unless the power to do so is included in the will. If you trust your personal representative, you can avoid the expense and delay of this by giving him or her the power to sell real estate without court approval.

Witnesses

A will must be witnessed by two persons to be valid. In all states except Vermont, only two witnesses are required.

In Florida (unlike some other states), it is legal for a beneficiary of a will to be a witness to the will. However, this is not a good idea, especially if there is anyone who may contest your will.

Self-Proving Affidavit

A will only needs two witnesses to be legal. If it includes a self-proving clause and is notarized, then the will can be admitted to probate quickly and there is no need to contact the witnesses. If it is not self-proved, then one of the witnesses must go to the courthouse and sign a statement that the will is genuine.

In an emergency situation—for example, if you are bedridden and there is no notary available—you can execute your will without the self-proving page. As long as it has two witnesses it will be valid. The only drawback is that at least one of the witnesses will later have to sign an oath.

Disinheriting Someone

Because it may result in your will being challenged in court, you should not make your own will if you intend to disinherit someone. However, you may wish to leave one child less than another because you already made a gift to that child or that child needs the money less than the other.

If you do give more to one child than to another, then you should state your reasons to show that you thought out your plan. Otherwise, the one who received less might argue that you did not realize what you were doing and were not competent to make a will.

Funeral Arrangements

There is no harm in stating your funeral preferences in your will, but in most states, directions for a funeral are not legally enforceable. Often a will is not found until after the funeral. Therefore it is better to tell your family about your wishes or to make prior arrangements yourself.

Handwritten Wills

In some states a person can hand write a will, without any witnesses, and it will be held valid. This is called a *holographic* will. In Florida, such a will is not valid unless it is signed in front of two witnesses, who must also sign it.

Forms

There are fourteen different will forms included in this book for easy use. You can either tear them out, photocopy them, or you can retype them on plain paper.

The forms in this book are printed on both sides of the page. If you photocopy them on separate pages or type your will on more than one piece of paper, you should staple the pages together, initial each page, and have both witnesses initial each page. Each page should state at the bottom—*page 1 of 3, page 2 of 3*, etc.

Corrections

Your will should have no white-outs or erasures. If for some reason it is impossible to make a will without corrections, they should be initialed by you and both witnesses.

4 HOW TO EXECUTE YOUR WILL

The signing of a will is a serious legal event and must be done properly or the will may be declared invalid. Preferably, it should be done in a private room without distraction. All parties must watch each other sign and no one should leave the scene until all have signed.

Example: Ebenezer was bedridden in a small room. His will was brought in to him to sign, but the witnesses could not actually see his hand signing because a dresser was in the way. His will was ignored by the court and his property went to two persons who were not in his will.

Procedure

To be sure your will is valid, you should follow these rules.

✪ You must state to your witnesses: *This is my will. I have read it and I understand it and this is how I want it to read. I want you two (or three) people to be my witnesses.* Contrary to popular belief, you do not have to read it to the witnesses or to let them read it.

✪   You must date your will and sign your name at the end in ink, exactly as it is printed in the will. Initial each page as both witnesses watch.

✪   You and the other witnesses must watch as each witness signs in ink and initials each page.

Self-Proving Affidavit

As explained in the last chapter, it is important to attach a self-proving affidavit to your will. This means that you will need to have a notary public present to watch everyone sign. If it is impossible to have a notary present, your will will still be valid, but the probate process may be delayed.

After your witnesses have signed as attesting witnesses under your name, you and they should sign the self-proving page and the notary should notarize it. The notary should *not* be one of your witnesses.

It is a good idea to make at least one copy of your will, but do not personally sign the copies or have them notarized. The reason for this is if you cancel or destroy your will, someone may produce one of the copies and have it probated or if you lose or destroy a copy, a court may assume you intended to revoke the original.

Example: Michael typed out a copy of his will and made two photocopies. He had the original and both copies signed and notarized. He then gave the original to his sister, who was his executor, and kept the two copies. Upon his death, the two copies were not found among his papers. Because these copies were in his possession and not found, it was assumed that he destroyed them. A court ruled that by destroying them he must have intended to revoke the original will, and his property went to persons not listed in his will.

Once you have prepared your will and properly executed it, you must make sure that it is kept in a safe place, where others can access it after death. You also may want to make changes to your will. These issues are discussed in this chapter.

Storing Your Will

Your will should be kept in a place safe from fire and easily accessible to your heirs. Your personal representative should know of its whereabouts. It can be kept in a home safe or fire box.

In some states, the opening of a safe deposit box in a bank after a person's death is a complicated affair. In Florida, however, a will can be removed from a safe deposit box easily, so you can keep it there.

If you are close to your children and can trust them explicitly, then you could allow one of them to keep the will in his or her safe deposit box. However, if you later decide to limit that child's share, there could be a problem.

Example: Diane made out her will giving her property to her two children equally and gave it to her older child, Bill, to hold. Years later, Bill moved away and her younger child, Mary, took care of her by coming over every day. Diane made a new will giving most her property to Mary. Upon Diane's death, Bill came to town and found the new will in Diane's house, but he destroyed it and probated the old will that gave him half the property.

Revoking Your Will

The usual way to revoke a will is to execute a new one that states that it revokes all previously made wills. To revoke a will without making a new one, you can tear, burn, cancel, deface, obliterate, or destroy it, as long as this is done with the intention of revoking it. If this is done accidentally, the will is not legally revoked.

Example: Ralph tells his son Clyde to go to the basement safe and tear up his (Ralph's) will. If Clyde does not tear it up in Ralph's presence, it is probably not effectively revoked.

Revival What if you change your will by drafting a new one and later decide you do not like the changes and want to go back to your old will? Can you destroy the new one and revive the old one? NO! Once you execute a new will—revoking an old will—you cannot revive the old will unless you execute a new document stating that you intend to revive the old will. In other words, you really should execute a new will.

Changing Your Will

You should not make any changes on your will after it has been signed. If you cross out a person's name or add a clause to a will that has already been signed, your change will not be valid and your entire will might become invalid.

One way to amend a will is to execute a *codicil*. A codicil is an amendment to a will. However, a codicil must be executed just like a will. It must have the same number of witnesses, and to be self-proved, it must include a self-proving page that must be notarized.

Because a codicil requires the same formality as a will, it is usually better to just make a new will.

In an emergency situation, if you want to change something in your will but cannot get to a notary to have it self-proved, you can execute a codicil that is witnessed but not self-proved. As long as it is properly witnessed (two witnesses) it will legally change your will. The only drawback would be that the witnesses would have to later sign an oath if it were not self-proved.

To prepare a codicil, use Form 18. To self-prove the codicil, use Form 19.

6 HOW TO MAKE A LIVING WILL

A living will is not a videotape of a person making a will. It has nothing to do with the usual type of will that distributes property. A living will is a document by which a person declares that he or she does not want artificial life support systems used if he or she becomes terminally ill.

Modern science can often keep a body alive even if the brain is permanently dead or if the person is in constant pain. In recent years, all states have legalized living wills either by statute or by court decision.

A living will must be signed in front of two witnesses who should not be blood relatives or a spouse. If the person is physically unable to sign, he or she may read the living will out loud and direct one of the witnesses to sign it for him or her. A living will can be in the form included in Florida statutes or it can be rewritten. But to be sure of its validity, it is best to use the statutory form.

Florida law also allows you to appoint a *designated health care surrogate* who can make health care decisions for you. For more information, see the *Florida Power of Attorney Handbook* by the publisher of this book.

The statutory living will form is included in Appendix B of this book as Form 20.

7 HOW TO MAKE ANATOMICAL GIFTS

Florida residents are allowed to donate their bodies or organs for research or transplantation. Consent may be given by a relative of a deceased person, but because relatives are often in shock or too upset to make such a decision, it is better to have one's intent made clear before death. This can be done by a statement in a will or by another signed document such as a **UNIFORM DONOR CARD**. The gift may be of all or part of one's body, and it may be made to a specific person, such as a physician or an ill relative.

The document making the donation must be signed before two witnesses who must also sign in each other's presence. If the donor cannot sign, then the document may be signed for him or her at his or her direction in the presence of the witnesses.

The donor may designate in the document who the physician is that will carry out the procedure.

If the document or will has been delivered to a specific donee, it may be amended or revoked by the donor in the following ways:

✪ by executing and delivering a signed statement to the donee;

✪ by an oral statement to two witnesses communicated to the donee;

✪ by an oral statement during a terminal illness made to an attending physician and communicated to the donee; or,

✪ by a signed document found on the person of the donor or in his or her effects.

If a document of gift has not been delivered to a donee, it may be revoked by any of the above methods or by destruction, cancellation, or mutilation of the document. It may also be revoked in the same method a will is revoked as described on page 34.

A **UNIFORM DONOR CARD** is included in Appendix B as Form 21. It must be signed in the presence of two signing witnesses.

GLOSSARY

A

administrator (*administratrix,* if female). A person appointed by the court to oversee distribution of the property of someone who died (either without a will, or if the person designated in the will is unable to serve).

attested will. A will that includes an attestation clause and has been signed in front of witnesses.

B

beneficiary. A person who is entitled to receive property from a person who died (regardless of whether there is a will).

bequest. Personal property left to someone in a will.

C

children's trust. A trust set up to hold property given to children. Usually it provides that the children will not receive their property until they reach a higher age than the age of majority.

codicil. An amendment to a will.

community property. Property acquired by a husband and wife by their labors during their marriage.

D

decedent. A person who has died.

descendent. A child, grandchild, great-grandchild, etc.

devise. Real property left to someone in a will. A person who is entitled to a devise is called a *devisee*.

E

elective share. In non-community property states, the portion of the estate which may be taken by a surviving spouse, regardless of what the will says.

executor (*executrix,* if female). A person appointed in a will to oversee distribution of the property of someone who died with a will. However, in Florida, this person is called a *personal representative*.

exempt property. Property that is exempt from distribution as a normal part of the estate.

F

family allowance. An amount of money set aside from the estate to support the family of the decedent for a period of time.

forced share. *See elective share.*

H

heir. A person who will inherit from a decedent who died without a will.

holographic will. A will in which all of the material provisions are entirely in the handwriting on the maker. Holographic wills are not legal in Florida.

I

intestate. Without making a will. One who dies without a will is said to have *died intestate.*

intestate share. In non-community property states, the portion of the estate a spouse is entitled to receive if there is no will.

J

joint tenancy. A type of property ownership by two or more persons, in which if one owner dies, that owner's interest goes to the other joint tenants (not to the deceased owner's heirs as in tenancy in common).

L

legacy. Real property left to someone in a will. A person who is entitled to a legacy is called a *legatee*.

living will. A document expressing the writer's desires regarding how medical care is to be handled in the event the writer is not able to express his or her wishes concerning the use of life-prolonging medical procedures.

P

per capita. Distribution of property with equal shares going to each person.

per stirpes. Distribution of property with equal shares going to each family line.

personal representative. A person appointed by the court, or will, to oversee distribution of the property of the person who died. This is a more modern term than administrator, executor, etc., and applies regardless of whether there is a will.

probate. The process of settling a decedent's estate through the probate court.

R

residue. The property that is left over in an estate after all specific bequests and devises.

S

self-proving affidavit. A form added to a will in which the will maker and witnesses state under oath that they have signed and witnessed the will.

specific bequest *or* **specific devise.** A gift in a will of a specific item of property or a specific amount of cash.

statutory will. A will that has been prepared according to the requirements of a statute.

T

tenancy by the entirety. A type of property ownership by a married couple in which the property automatically passes to one spouse upon the death of the other. This is basically the same as joint tenancy, except that it is only between a husband and wife.

tenancy in common. Ownership of property by two or more people in which each owner's share would descend to that owner's heirs (not to the other owners as in joint tenancy).

testate. With a will. One who dies with a will is said to have *died testate*.

testator (*testatrix,* if female). A person who makes his or her will.

APPENDIX A:
SAMPLE FILLED-IN FORMS

The following pages include sample filled-in forms for some of the wills in this book. They are filled out in different ways for different situations. You should look at all of them to see how the different sections can be filled in. Only one example of a self-proved will affidavit is shown, but you should use it with every will.

Last Will and Testament

I, _____John Smith_____ a resident of _____Dade_____ County, Florida do hereby make, publish, and declare this to be my Last Will and Testament, hereby revoking any and all Wills and Codicils heretofore made by me.

FIRST: I direct that all my just debts and funeral expenses be paid out of my estate as soon after my death as is practicable.

SECOND: I may leave a statement or list disposing of certain items of my tangible personal property. Any such statement or list in existence at the time of my death shall be determinative with respect to all items bequeathed therein.

THIRD: I give, devise, and bequeath all my estate, real, personal, and mixed, of whatever kind and wherever situated, of which I may die seized or possessed, or in which I may have any interest or over which I may have any power of appointment or testamentary disposition, to my spouse, _____Barbara Smith_____. If my said spouse does not survive me, I give, and bequeath the said property to _____my sisters, Jan Smith, Joan Smith, and Jennifer Smith in equal shares-------------_____

_____

or the survivor of them.

FOURTH: In the event that any beneficiary fails to survive me by thirty days, then this will shall take effect as if that person had predeceased me.

FIFTH: I hereby nominate, constitute, and appoint _____Barbara Smith_____ as Personal Representative of this, my Last Will and Testament. In the event that such named person is unable or unwilling to serve at any time or for any reason, then I nominate, constitute, and appoint _____Reginald Smith_____ as Personal Representative in the place and stead of the person first named herein. It is my will and I direct that my Personal Representative shall not be required to furnish a bond for the faithful performance of his or her duties in any jurisdiction, any provision of law to the contrary notwithstanding, and I give my Personal Representative full power to administer my estate, including the power to settle claims, pay debts, and sell, lease or exchange real and personal property without court order.

IN WITNESS WHEREOF I declare this to be my Last Will and Testament and execute it willingly as my free and voluntary act for the purposes expressed herein and I am of legal age and sound mind and make this under no constraint or undue influence, this _29th_ day of _July_, _2004_ at _Miami Beach_ State of _Florida_.

_____*John Smith*_____ L.S.

The foregoing instrument was on said date subscribed at the end thereof by _____John Smith_____, the above named Testator who signed, published, and declared this instrument to be his/her Last Will and Testament in the presence of us and each of us, who thereupon at his/her request, in his/her presence, and in the presence of each other, have hereunto subscribed our names as witnesses thereto. We are of sound mind and proper age to witness a will and understand this to be his/her will, and to the best of our knowledge testator is of legal age to make a will, of sound mind, and under no constraint or undue influence.

__*Brenda Jones*_____residing at___West Palm Beach, Florida_____

__*John Doe*_____residing at___Key Largo, Florida_____

Last Will and Testament

I, _____John Smith_____ a resident of __Hillsborough__
County, Florida do hereby make, publish, and declare this to be my Last Will and Testament, hereby
revoking any and all Wills and Codicils heretofore made by me.

FIRST: I direct that all my just debts and funeral expenses be paid out of my estate as soon
after my death as is practicable.

SECOND: I may leave a statement or list disposing of certain items of my tangible personal
property. Any such statement or list in existence at the time of my death shall be determinative with
respect to all items bequeathed therein.

THIRD: I give, devise, and bequeath all my estate, real, personal, and mixed, of whatever kind and
wherever situated, of which I may die seized or possessed, or in which I may have any interest or over
which I may have any power of appointment or testamentary disposition, to my spouse,
_____Barbara Smith_____. If my said spouse does not survive me, I give,
and bequeath the said property to my children _____Amy Smith and Sammy Smith_____
_____
_____
in equal shares or to their lineal descendants, per stirpes.

FOURTH: In the event that any beneficiary fails to survive me by thirty days, then this will
shall take effect as if that person had predeceased me.

FIFTH: I hereby nominate, constitute, and appoint _____Barbara Smith_____ as
Personal Representative of this, my Last Will and Testament. In the event that such named person is
unable or unwilling to serve at any time or for any reason, then I nominate, constitute, and appoint
_____Reginald Smith_____ as Personal Representative in the place and stead of the person first named herein. It is my will and I direct that my Personal Representative shall not be required
to furnish a bond for the faithful performance of his or her duties in any jurisdiction, any provision
of law to the contrary notwithstanding, and I give my Personal Representative full power to administer my estate, including the power to settle claims, pay debts, and sell, lease or exchange real and
personal property without court order.

IN WITNESS WHEREOF I declare this to be my Last Will and Testament and execute it willingly as my free and voluntary act for the purposes expressed herein and I am of legal age and sound
mind and make this under no constraint or undue influence, this _29th_ day of _____July, 2004_ at
_____Tampa_____ State of _____Florida_____.

_____*John Smith*_____L.S.

The foregoing instrument was on said date subscribed at the end thereof by
_____John Smith_____, the above named Testator who signed, published,
and declared this instrument to be his/her Last Will and Testament in the presence of us and each of

us, who thereupon at his/her request, in his/her presence, and in the presence of each other, have hereunto subscribed our names as witnesses thereto. We are of sound mind and proper age to witness a will and understand this to be his/her will, and to the best of our knowledge testator is of legal age to make a will, of sound mind, and under no constraint or undue influence.

_____*Brenda Jones*_____residing at_____Tampa, Florida_____

_____*John Doe*_____residing at_____Key West, Florida_____

Last Will and Testament

I, _____John Smith_____ a resident of _Escambia_____ County, Florida do hereby make, publish, and declare this to be my Last Will and Testament, hereby revoking any and all Wills and Codicils heretofore made by me.

FIRST: I direct that all my just debts and funeral expenses be paid out of my estate as soon after my death as is practicable.

SECOND: I may leave a statement or list disposing of certain items of my tangible personal property. Any such statement or list in existence at the time of my death shall be determinative with respect to all items bequeathed therein.

THIRD: I give, devise, and bequeath all my estate, real, personal, and mixed, of whatever kind and wherever situated, of which I may die seized or possessed, or in which I may have any interest or over which I may have any power of appointment or testamentary disposition, to my children _____Franny Smith, Zooey Smith, Holden Smith ----_____

_____

_____,

plus any afterborn or adopted children in equal shares or to their lineal descendants per stirpes.

FOURTH: In the event that any beneficiary fails to survive me by thirty days, then this will shall take effect as if that person had predeceased me.

FIFTH: In the event any of my children have not attained the age of 18 years at the time of my death, I hereby nominate, constitute, and appoint _____Taylor Smith_____ as guardian over the person of any of my children who have not reached the age of majority at the time of my death. In the event that said guardian is unable or unwilling to serve, then I nominate, constitute, and appoint _____Nathan Smith_____ as guardian. Said guardian shall serve without bond or surety.

SIXTH: In the event any of my children have not attained the age of 18 years at the time of my death, I hereby nominate, constitute, and appoint _____Taylor Smith_____ as guardian over the property of any of my children who have not reached the age of majority at the time of my death. In the event that said guardian is unable or unwilling to serve, then I nominate, constitute, and appoint _____Nathan Smith_____ as guardian. Said guardian shall serve without bond or surety.

SEVENTH: I hereby nominate, constitute, and appoint __Morgan Smith_____ as Personal Representative of this, my Last Will and Testament. In the event that such named person is unable or unwilling to serve at any time or for any reason, then I nominate, constitute, and appoint _____Courtney Smith_____ as Personal Representative in the place and stead of the person first named herein. It is my will and I direct that my Personal Representative shall not be required to furnish a bond for the faithful performance of his or her duties in any jurisdiction, any provision of law to the contrary notwithstanding, and I give my Personal Representative full power to administer my estate, including the power to settle claims, pay debts, and sell, lease or exchange real and personal property without court order.

IN WITNESS WHEREOF I declare this to be my Last Will and Testament and execute it willingly as my free and voluntary act for the purposes expressed herein and I am of legal age and sound mind and make this under no constraint or undue influence, this <u>22nd</u> day of <u>July</u>, <u>2004</u> at <u>Key Largo</u> State of <u>Florida</u>.

John Smith   L.S.

The foregoing instrument was on said date subscribed at the end thereof by <u>John Smith</u>, the above named Testator who signed, published, and declared this instrument to be his/her Last Will and Testament in the presence of us and each of us, who thereupon at his/her request, in his/her presence, and in the presence of each other, have hereunto subscribed our names as witnesses thereto. We are of sound mind and proper age to witness a will and understand this to be his/her will, and to the best of our knowledge testator is of legal age to make a will, of sound mind, and under no constraint or undue influence.

Donny Roe residing at Pensacola, Florida

Melvin Coe residing at Pensacola, Florida

Last Will and Testament

I, _____Mary Smith_____ a resident of __Levy_____
County, Florida do hereby make, publish, and declare this to be my Last Will and Testament, hereby revoking any and all Wills and Codicils heretofore made by me.

FIRST: I direct that all my just debts and funeral expenses be paid out of my estate as soon after my death as is practicable.

SECOND: I may leave a statement or list disposing of certain items of my tangible personal property. Any such statement or list in existence at the time of my death shall be determinative with respect to all items bequeathed therein.

THIRD: I give, devise, and bequeath all my estate, real, personal, and mixed, of whatever kind and wherever situated, of which I may die seized or possessed, or in which I may have any interest or over which I may have any power of appointment or testamentary disposition, to the following: __my brothers John Smith, Paul Smith, and George Smith -----_____

_____

_____,

or to the survivor of them.

FOURTH: In the event that any beneficiary fails to survive me by thirty days, then this will shall take effect as if that person had predeceased me.

FIFTH: I hereby nominate, constitute, and appoint __Susan Doe_____ as Personal Representative of this, my Last Will and Testament. In the event that such named person is unable or unwilling to serve at any time or for any reason, then I nominate, constitute, and appoint ____Aaron Doe_____ as Personal Representative in the place and stead of the person first named herein. It is my will and I direct that my Personal Representative shall not be required to furnish a bond for the faithful performance of his or her duties in any jurisdiction, any provision of law to the contrary notwithstanding, and I give my Personal Representative full power to administer my estate, including the power to settle claims, pay debts, and sell, lease or exchange real and personal property without court order.

IN WITNESS WHEREOF I declare this to be my Last Will and Testament and execute it willingly as my free and voluntary act for the purposes expressed herein and I am of legal age and sound mind and make this under no constraint or undue influence, this __1st__ day of __December_____, __2004__ at __Chiefland_____ State of __Florida_____.

_____*Mary Smith*_____L.S.

The foregoing instrument was on said date subscribed at the end thereof by _____Mary Smith_____, the above named Testator who signed, published, and declared this instrument to be his/her Last Will and Testament in the presence of us and each of us, who thereupon at his/her request, in his/her presence, and in the presence of each other, have hereunto subscribed our names as witnesses thereto. We are of sound mind and proper age to witness a will and understand this to be his/her will, and to the best of our knowledge testator is of legal age to make a will, of sound mind, and under no constraint or undue influence.

Leon Brown _____residing at___ Otter Creek, Florida _____

Melvina Brown _____residing at___ Otter Creek, Florida _____

Self-Proved Will Affidavit
(attach to Will)

STATE OF FLORIDA
COUNTY OF ___Pinellas_____

I,___John Doe_____, declare to the officer taking my acknowledgment of this instrument, and to the subscribing witnesses, that I signed this instrument as my will.

*John Doe*_____
Testator

We, ___Jane Roe_____ and ___Melvin Coe_____, have been sworn by the officer signing below, and declare to that officer on our oaths that the testator declared the instrument to be the testator's will and signed it in our presence and that we each signed the instrument as a witness in the presence of the testator and of each other.

*Jane Roe*_____
Witness

*Melvin Coe*_____
Witness

Acknowledged and subscribed before me by the testator, ___John Doe_____ who is personally known to me or who has produced ___Fl.Dr. Lic. D1234567890___ as identification, and sworn to and subscribed before me by the witnesses, ___Jane Roe_____ who is personally known to me or who has produced ___Fl.Dr. Lic. D5678901234___ as identification and ___Melvin Coe_____ who is personally known to me or who has produced ___Fl.Dr. Lic. D7890123456___ as identification, and subscribed by me in the presence of the testator and the subscribing witnesses, all on ___September 1st___, 20_04_.

*C. U. Sine*_____
Notary or other officer

Codicil to the Will of

<u>Larry Lowe</u>

I, <u>Larry Lowe</u>, a resident of <u>Leon</u> County, Florida declare this to be the first codicil to my Last Will and Testament dated <u>July 5</u>, <u>2004</u>.

    FIRST: I hereby revoke the clause of my Will which reads as follows: <u>FOURTH: I hearby leave $5,000.00 to my daughter Mildred</u>

    SECOND: I hereby add the following clause to my Will: <u>FOURTH: I hearby leave $1,000.00 to my daughter Mildred</u>

    THIRD: In all other respects I hereby confirm and republish my Last Will and Testament dated <u>July 5</u>, <u>2004</u>.

    IN WITNESS WHEREOF, I have signed, published, and declared the foregoing instrument as and for a codicil to my Last Will and Testament, this <u>5th</u> day of <u>January</u>, <u>2005</u>.

Larry Lowe

    The foregoing instrument was on the <u>5th</u> day of <u>January</u>, <u>2005</u>, signed at the end thereof, and at the same time published and declared by <u>Larry Lowe</u>, as and for a codicil to his/her Last Will and Testament, dated <u>July 5</u>, <u>2004</u>, in the presence of each of us, who, this attestation clause having been read to us, did at the request of the said testator/testatrix, in his/her presence and in the presence of each other signed our names as witnesses thereto.

James Smith   residing at <u>Tallahassee, Florida</u>

Mary Smith   residing at <u>Tallahassee, Florida</u>

Living Will

Declaration made this 5th day of _____ October _____ , _2004_ . I,
__Norman Milquetoast__ , willfully and voluntarily make known my desire that my dying not be artificially prolonged under the circumstances set forth below, and I do hereby declare:

If at any time I have a terminal condition and if my attending or treating physician and another consulting physician have determined that there can be no medical probability of my recovery from such condition, I direct that life-prolonging procedures be withheld or withdrawn when the application of such procedures would serve only to prolong artificially the process of dying, and that I be permitted to die naturally with only the administration of medication or the performance of any medical procedure deemed necessary to provide me with comfort, care or alleviate pain.

It is my intention that this declaration be honored by my family and physician as the final expression of my legal right to refuse medical or surgical treatment and to accept the consequences for such refusal.

In the event that I have been determined to be unable to provide express and informed consent regarding the withholding, withdrawal, or continuation of life-prolonging procedures, I wish to designate, as my surrogate to carry out the provisions of this declaration:

Name:__ Beatrice Milquetoast _____

Address:__ 1234 Florida Avenue _____

__ Winter Haven, FL _____ Zip Code:__ 33210 _____

Phone: ___ (407) 555-1212 _____

I understand the full import of this declaration, and am emotionally and mentally competent to make this declaration.

Additional instructions (optional):

_____

_____

	__*Norman Milquetoast*__
	(Signed)
__*Harvey Nabor*__	__*June Nabor*__
Witness	Witness
__1236 Florida Avenue__	__1236 Florida Avenue__
Address	Address
__Winter Haven, FL 33210__	__Winter Haven, FL 33210__
__(407) 555-2121__	__(407) 555-2121__
Phone	Phone

APPENDIX B:
BLANK FORMS

The following pages contain forms that can be used to prepare a will, codicil, living will, and donor cards. They should only be used by persons who have read this book, who do not have any complications in their legal affairs and who understand the forms they are using. The forms may be used right out of the book or they may be photocopied or retyped.

How to Pick the Right Will

Follow the chart and use the form number in the black circle,
then use Form 17, the self-proving affidavit.

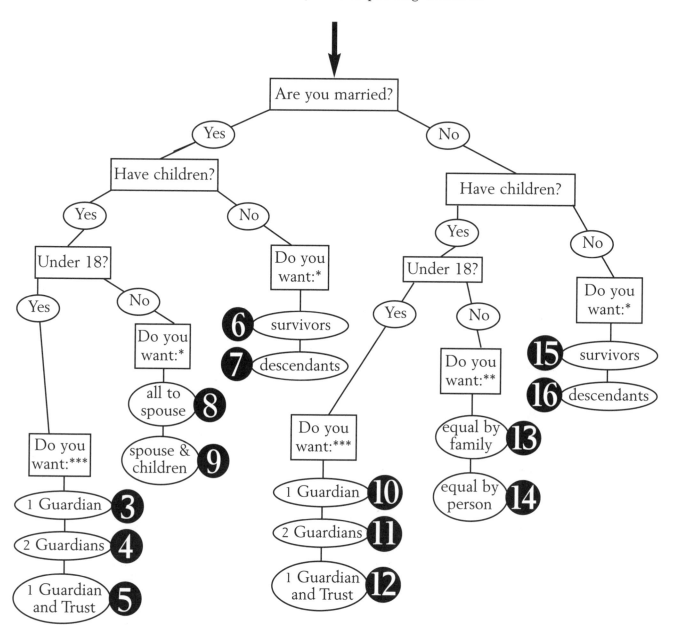

17 Be sure to use Form 17, the self-proving affidavit with your will, no matter which form you use.

* For an explanation of survivors/descendants, see page 24.
** For an explanation of families/persons, see page 25.
*** For an explanation of children's guardians and trust, see pages 26–27.

Asset and Beneficiary List

Property Inventory

Assets

Bank Accounts (checking, savings, certificates of deposit)

_____
_____
_____
_____
_____
_____
_____
_____

Real Estate

_____
_____
_____
_____
_____
_____
_____
_____

Vehicles (cars, trucks, boats, planes, RVs, etc.)

_____
_____
_____
_____
_____
_____
_____

Personal Property (collections, jewelry, tools, artwork, household items, etc.)

_____
_____
_____
_____
_____
_____
_____

_____
_____
_____
_____
_____
_____
_____

Stocks/Bonds/Mutual Funds

_____
_____
_____
_____
_____
_____
_____
_____
_____
_____
_____
_____
_____
_____

Retirement Accounts (IRAs, 401(k)s, pension plans, etc.)

_____
_____
_____
_____
_____
_____
_____

Receivables (mortgages held, notes, accounts receivable, personal loans)

_____
_____
_____
_____
_____
_____

Life Insurance

_____

_____

_____

_____

_____

_____

_____

Other Property (trusts, partnerships, businesses, profit sharing, copyrights, etc.)

_____

_____

_____

_____

_____

_____

_____

Liabilities

Real Estate Loans

_____

_____

_____

_____

_____

_____

_____

Vehicle Loans

_____

_____

_____

_____

_____

_____

_____

Other Secured Loans

_____
_____
_____
_____
_____
_____
_____
_____

Unsecured Loans and Debts (taxes, child support, judgments, etc.)

_____
_____
_____
_____
_____
_____
_____
_____

Beneficiary List

Name_____ Address_____ Phone_____

_____
_____
_____
_____
_____
_____
_____
_____

Preferences and Information List

STATEMENT OF DESIRES AND LOCATION OF PROPERTY & DOCUMENTS

I, _____, am signing this document as the expression of my desires as to the matters stated below, and to inform my family members or other significant persons of the location of certain property and documents in the event of any emergency or of my death.

1.   **Funeral Desires.** It is my desire that the following arrangements be made for my funeral and disposition of remains in the event of my death (state if you have made any arrangements, such as pre-paid burial plans, cemetery plots owned, etc.):

❑   Burial at _____
     _____.

❑   Cremation at _____
     _____.

❑   Other specific desires: _____
     _____
     _____.

2.   **Pets.** I have the following pet(s): _____
_____. The following are my desires concerning the
care of said pet(s): _____
_____
_____.

4.   **Notification.** I would like the following person(s) notified in the event of emergency or death (give name, address and phone number):

_____
_____
_____
_____
_____

5.   **Location of Documents.** The following is a list of important documents, and their location:

❑   Last Will and Testament, dated _____. Location: _____
     _____.

❑   Durable Power of Attorney, dated _____. Location: _____
     _____.

❑   Living Will, dated _____. Location: _____
     _____.

❑   Deed(s) to real estate (describe property location and location of deed):
     _____
     _____
     _____

❑ Title(s) to vehicles (cars, boats, etc.) (Describe vehicle, its location, and location of title, registration, or other documents):

_____
_____
_____
_____

❑ Life insurance policies (list name address & phone number of insurance company and insurance agent, policy number, and location of policy):

_____
_____
_____
_____

❑ Other insurance policies (list type, company & agent, policy number, and location of policy):

_____
_____
_____

❑ Other: (list other documents such as stock certificates, bonds, certificates of deposit, etc., and their location):

_____
_____
_____
_____

6.   **Location of Assets.** In addition to items readily visible in my home or listed above, I have the following assets:

❑ Safe deposit box located at _____, box number _____. Key located at: _____.

❑ Bank accounts (list name & address of bank, type of account, and account number):

_____

❑ Other (describe the item and give its location):

_____
_____
_____
_____
_____

7.   Other desires or information (state any desires or provide any information not given above; use additional sheets of paper if necessary):

_____
_____
_____
_____
_____

Dated: _____

_____
Signature

Last Will and Testament

I, _____ a resident of _____
County, Florida do hereby make, publish, and declare this to be my Last Will and Testament, hereby
revoking any and all Wills and Codicils heretofore made by me.

FIRST: I direct that all my just debts and funeral expenses be paid out of my estate as soon
after my death as is practicable.

SECOND: I may leave a statement or list disposing of certain items of my tangible personal
property. Any such statement or list in existence at the time of my death shall be determinative with
respect to all items bequeathed therein.

THIRD: I give, devise, and bequeath all my estate, real, personal, and mixed, of whatever
kind and wherever situated, of which I may die seized or possessed, or in which I may have any
interest or over which I may have any power of appointment or testamentary disposition, to my
spouse, _____. If my said spouse does not survive me,
I give, and bequeath the said property to my children _____
_____
_____,
plus any afterborn or adopted children in equal shares or their lineal descendants, per stirpes.

FOURTH: In the event that any beneficiary fails to survive me by thirty days, then this will
shall take effect as if that person had predeceased me.

FIFTH: Should my spouse not survive me, I hereby nominate, constitute, and appoint
_____ as guardian over the person and estate of any of
my children who have not reached the age of majority at the time of my death. In the event that said
guardian is unable or unwilling to serve, then I nominate, constitute, and appoint
_____ as guardian. Said guardian shall serve without bond
or surety.

SIXTH: I hereby nominate, constitute, and appoint _____
as Personal Representative of this, my Last Will and Testament. In the event that such named person is unable or unwilling to serve at any time or for any reason, then I nominate, constitute, and
appoint _____ as Personal Representative in the place and stead of
the person first named herein. It is my will and I direct that my Personal Representative shall not be
required to furnish a bond for the faithful performance of his or her duties in any jurisdiction, any
provision of law to the contrary notwithstanding, and I give my Personal Representative full power
to administer my estate, including the power to settle claims, pay debts, and sell, lease or exchange
real and personal property without court order.

IN WITNESS WHEREOF I declare this to be my Last Will and Testament and execute it willingly as my free and voluntary act for the purposes expressed herein and I am of legal age and sound mind and make this under no constraint or undue influence, this _____ day of _____, _____ at _____ State of _____.

_____L.S.

The foregoing instrument was on said date subscribed at the end thereof by _____, the above named Testator who signed, published, and declared this instrument to be his/her Last Will and Testament in the presence of us and each of us, who thereupon at his/her request, in his/her presence, and in the presence of each other, have hereunto subscribed our names as witnesses thereto. We are of sound mind and proper age to witness a will and understand this to be his/her will, and to the best of our knowledge testator is of legal age to make a will, of sound mind, and under no constraint or undue influence.

_____residing at_____

_____residing at_____

Last Will and Testament

I, _____ a resident of _____
County, Florida do hereby make, publish, and declare this to be my Last Will and Testament, hereby
revoking any and all Wills and Codicils heretofore made by me.

FIRST: I direct that all my just debts and funeral expenses be paid out of my estate as soon
after my death as is practicable.

SECOND: I may leave a statement or list disposing of certain items of my tangible personal
property. Any such statement or list in existence at the time of my death shall be determinative with
respect to all items bequeathed therein.

THIRD: I give, devise, and bequeath all my estate, real, personal, and mixed, of whatever
kind and wherever situated, of which I may die seized or possessed, or in which I may have any
interest or over which I may have any power of appointment or testamentary disposition, to my
spouse, _____. If my said spouse does not survive me,
I give, and bequeath the said property to my children _____
_____
_____,
plus any afterborn or adopted children in equal shares or their lineal descendants, per stirpes.

FOURTH: In the event that any beneficiary fails to survive me by thirty days, then this will
shall take effect as if that person had predeceased me.

FIFTH: Should my spouse not survive me, I hereby nominate, constitute, and appoint
_____, as guardian over the person of any of my children who
have not reached the age of majority at the time of my death. In the event that said guardian is unable
or unwilling to serve, then I nominate, constitute, and appoint _____
as guardian. Said guardian shall serve without bond or surety.

SIXTH: Should my spouse not survive me, I hereby nominate, constitute, and appoint
_____ as guardian over the estate of any of my children who have
not reached the age of majority at the time of my death. In the event that said guardian is unable or
unwilling to serve, then I nominate, constitute, and appoint _____
as guardian. Said guardian shall serve without bond or surety.

SEVENTH: I hereby nominate, constitute, and appoint _____
as Personal Representative of this, my Last Will and Testament. In the event that such named person is unable or unwilling to serve at any time or for any reason, then I nominate, constitute, and
appoint _____ as Personal Representative in the place and stead of
the person first named herein. It is my will and I direct that my Personal Representative shall not be
required to furnish a bond for the faithful performance of his or her duties in any jurisdiction, any
provision of law to the contrary notwithstanding, and I give my Personal Representative full power
to administer my estate, including the power to settle claims, pay debts, and sell, lease or exchange
real and personal property without court order.

IN WITNESS WHEREOF I declare this to be my Last Will and Testament and execute it willingly as my free and voluntary act for the purposes expressed herein and I am of legal age and sound mind and make this under no constraint or undue influence, this _____ day of _____, _____ at _____ State of _____.

_____L.S.

The foregoing instrument was on said date subscribed at the end thereof by _____, the above named Testator who signed, published, and declared this instrument to be his/her Last Will and Testament in the presence of us and each of us, who thereupon at his/her request, in his/her presence, and in the presence of each other, have hereunto subscribed our names as witnesses thereto. We are of sound mind and proper age to witness a will and understand this to be his/her will, and to the best of our knowledge testator is of legal age to make a will, of sound mind, and under no constraint or undue influence.

_____residing at_____

_____residing at_____

Last Will and Testament

I, _____ a resident of _____
County, Florida do hereby make, publish, and declare this to be my Last Will and Testament, hereby
revoking any and all Wills and Codicils heretofore made by me.

FIRST: I direct that all my just debts and funeral expenses be paid out of my estate as soon
after my death as is practicable.

SECOND: I may leave a statement or list disposing of certain items of my tangible personal
property. Any such statement or list in existence at the time of my death shall be determinative with
respect to all items bequeathed therein.

THIRD: I give, devise, and bequeath all my estate, real, personal, and mixed, of whatever
kind and wherever situated, of which I may die seized or possessed, or in which I may have any
interest or over which I may have any power of appointment or testamentary disposition, to my
spouse, _____. If my said spouse does not survive me,
I give, and bequeath the said property to my children _____
_____
_____,
plus any afterborn or adopted children in equal shares or their lineal descendants, per stirpes.

FOURTH: In the event that any beneficiary fails to survive me by thirty days, then this will
shall take effect as if that person had predeceased me.

FIFTH: In the event that any of my children have not reached the age of _____ years at
the time of my death, then the share of any such child shall be held in a separate trust by
_____ for such child.

The trustee shall use the income and that part of the principal of the trust as is, in the trustee's sole
discretion, necessary or desirable to provide proper housing, medical care, food, clothing, entertainment and education for the trust beneficiary, considering the beneficiary's other resources. Any
income that is not distributed shall be added to the principal. Additionally, the trustee shall have all
powers conferred by the law of the state having jurisdiction over this trust, as well as the power to
pay from the assets of the trust reasonable fees necessary to administer the trust.

The trust shall terminate when the child reaches the age specified above and the remaining assets
distributed to the child, unless they have been exhausted sooner. In the event the child dies prior to
the termination of the trust, then the assets shall pass to the estate of the child. The interests of the
beneficiary under this trust shall not be assignable and shall be free from the claims of creditors to
the full extent allowed by law.

In the event the said trustee is unable or unwilling to serve for any reason, then I nominate, constitute, and appoint _____ as alternate trustee. No bond

shall be required of either trustee in any jurisdiction and this trust shall be administered without court supervision as allowed by law.

SIXTH: Should my spouse not survive me, I hereby nominate, constitute, and appoint _____ as guardian over the person and estate of any of my children who have not reached the age of majority at the time of my death. In the event that said guardian is unable or unwilling to serve, then I nominate, constitute, and appoint _____ as guardian.

SEVENTH: I hereby nominate, constitute, and appoint _____ as Personal Representative of this, my Last Will and Testament. In the event that such named person is unable or unwilling to serve at any time or for any reason, then I nominate, constitute, and appoint _____ as Personal Representative in the place and stead of the person first named herein. It is my will and I direct that my Personal Representative shall not be required to furnish a bond for the faithful performance of his or her duties in any jurisdiction, any provision of law to the contrary notwithstanding, and I give my Personal Representative full power to administer my estate, including the power to settle claims, pay debts, and sell, lease or exchange real and personal property without court order.

IN WITNESS WHEREOF I declare this to be my Last Will and Testament and execute it willingly as my free and voluntary act for the purposes expressed herein and I am of legal age and sound mind and make this under no constraint or undue influence, this _____ day of _____, _____ at _____ State of _____.

_____ L.S.

The foregoing instrument was on said date subscribed at the end thereof by _____, the above named Testator who signed, published, and declared this instrument to be his/her Last Will and Testament in the presence of us and each of us, who thereupon at his/her request, in his/her presence, and in the presence of each other, have hereunto subscribed our names as witnesses thereto. We are of sound mind and proper age to witness a will and understand this to be his/her will, and to the best of our knowledge testator is of legal age to make a will, of sound mind, and under no constraint or undue influence.

_____ residing at _____

_____ residing at _____

Last Will and Testament

I, _____ a resident of _____ County, Florida do hereby make, publish, and declare this to be my Last Will and Testament, hereby revoking any and all Wills and Codicils heretofore made by me.

FIRST: I direct that all my just debts and funeral expenses be paid out of my estate as soon after my death as is practicable.

SECOND: I may leave a statement or list disposing of certain items of my tangible personal property. Any such statement or list in existence at the time of my death shall be determinative with respect to all items bequeathed therein.

THIRD: I give, devise, and bequeath all my estate, real, personal, and mixed, of whatever kind and wherever situated, of which I may die seized or possessed, or in which I may have any interest or over which I may have any power of appointment or testamentary disposition, to my spouse, _____. If my said spouse does not survive me, I give, and bequeath the said property to _____ _____ _____, or the survivor of them.

FOURTH: In the event that any beneficiary fails to survive me by thirty days, then this will shall take effect as if that person had predeceased me.

FIFTH: I hereby nominate, constitute, and appoint _____ as Personal Representative of this, my Last Will and Testament. In the event that such named person is unable or unwilling to serve at any time or for any reason, then I nominate, constitute, and appoint _____ as Personal Representative in the place and stead of the person first named herein. It is my will and I direct that my Personal Representative shall not be required to furnish a bond for the faithful performance of his or her duties in any jurisdiction, any provision of law to the contrary notwithstanding, and I give my Personal Representative full power to administer my estate, including the power to settle claims, pay debts, and sell, lease or exchange real and personal property without court order.

IN WITNESS WHEREOF I declare this to be my Last Will and Testament and execute it willingly as my free and voluntary act for the purposes expressed herein and I am of legal age and sound mind and make this under no constraint or undue influence, this _____ day of _____, _____ at _____ State of _____.

_____L.S.

The foregoing instrument was on said date subscribed at the end thereof by
_____, the above named Testator who signed, published,
and declared this instrument to be his/her Last Will and Testament in the presence of us and each of
us, who thereupon at his/her request, in his/her presence, and in the presence of each other, have
hereunto subscribed our names as witnesses thereto. We are of sound mind and proper age to witness a will and understand this to be his/her will, and to the best of our knowledge testator is of legal
age to make a will, of sound mind, and under no constraint or undue influence.

_____residing at_____

_____residing at_____

Last Will and Testament

I, _____ a resident of _____
County, Florida do hereby make, publish, and declare this to be my Last Will and Testament, hereby revoking any and all Wills and Codicils heretofore made by me.

FIRST: I direct that all my just debts and funeral expenses be paid out of my estate as soon after my death as is practicable.

SECOND: I may leave a statement or list disposing of certain items of my tangible personal property. Any such statement or list in existence at the time of my death shall be determinative with respect to all items bequeathed therein.

THIRD: I give, devise, and bequeath all my estate, real, personal, and mixed, of whatever kind and wherever situated, of which I may die seized or possessed, or in which I may have any interest or over which I may have any power of appointment or testamentary disposition, to my spouse, _____. If my said spouse does not survive me, I give, and bequeath the said property to _____
_____
_____,
or to their lineal descendants, per stirpes.

FOURTH: In the event that any beneficiary fails to survive me by thirty days, then this will shall take effect as if that person had predeceased me.

FIFTH: I hereby nominate, constitute, and appoint _____ as Personal Representative of this, my Last Will and Testament. In the event that such named person is unable or unwilling to serve at any time or for any reason, then I nominate, constitute, and appoint _____ as Personal Representative in the place and stead of the person first named herein. It is my will and I direct that my Personal Representative shall not be required to furnish a bond for the faithful performance of his or her duties in any jurisdiction, any provision of law to the contrary notwithstanding, and I give my Personal Representative full power to administer my estate, including the power to settle claims, pay debts, and sell, lease or exchange real and personal property without court order.

IN WITNESS WHEREOF I declare this to be my Last Will and Testament and execute it willingly as my free and voluntary act for the purposes expressed herein and I am of legal age and sound mind and make this under no constraint or undue influence, this _____ day of _____, _____ at _____ State of _____.

_____L.S.

    The foregoing instrument was on said date subscribed at the end thereof by _____, the above named Testator who signed, published, and declared this instrument to be his/her Last Will and Testament in the presence of us and each of us, who thereupon at his/her request, in his/her presence, and in the presence of each other, have hereunto subscribed our names as witnesses thereto. We are of sound mind and proper age to witness a will and understand this to be his/her will, and to the best of our knowledge testator is of legal age to make a will, of sound mind, and under no constraint or undue influence.

_____residing at_____

_____residing at_____

Last Will and Testament

I, _____ a resident of _____ County, Florida do hereby make, publish, and declare this to be my Last Will and Testament, hereby revoking any and all Wills and Codicils heretofore made by me.

FIRST: I direct that all my just debts and funeral expenses be paid out of my estate as soon after my death as is practicable.

SECOND: I may leave a statement or list disposing of certain items of my tangible personal property. Any such statement or list in existence at the time of my death shall be determinative with respect to all items bequeathed therein.

THIRD: I give, devise, and bequeath all my estate, real, personal, and mixed, of whatever kind and wherever situated, of which I may die seized or possessed, or in which I may have any interest or over which I may have any power of appointment or testamentary disposition, to my spouse, _____. If my said spouse does not survive me, I give, and bequeath the said property to my children _____ _____ _____, in equal shares or to their lineal descendants, per stirpes.

FOURTH: In the event that any beneficiary fails to survive me by thirty days, then this will shall take effect as if that person had predeceased me.

FIFTH: I hereby nominate, constitute, and appoint _____ as Personal Representative of this, my Last Will and Testament. In the event that such named person is unable or unwilling to serve at any time or for any reason, then I nominate, constitute, and appoint _____ as Personal Representative in the place and stead of the person first named herein. It is my will and I direct that my Personal Representative shall not be required to furnish a bond for the faithful performance of his or her duties in any jurisdiction, any provision of law to the contrary notwithstanding, and I give my Personal Representative full power to administer my estate, including the power to settle claims, pay debts, and sell, lease or exchange real and personal property without court order.

IN WITNESS WHEREOF I declare this to be my Last Will and Testament and execute it willingly as my free and voluntary act for the purposes expressed herein and I am of legal age and sound mind and make this under no constraint or undue influence, this _____ day of _____, _____ at _____ State of _____.

_____L.S.

The foregoing instrument was on said date subscribed at the end thereof by
_____, the above named Testator who signed, published,
and declared this instrument to be his/her Last Will and Testament in the presence of us and each of
us, who thereupon at his/her request, in his/her presence, and in the presence of each other, have
hereunto subscribed our names as witnesses thereto. We are of sound mind and proper age to witness a will and understand this to be his/her will, and to the best of our knowledge testator is of legal
age to make a will, of sound mind, and under no constraint or undue influence.

_____ residing at _____

_____ residing at _____

Last Will and Testament

I, _____ a resident of _____ County, Florida do hereby make, publish, and declare this to be my Last Will and Testament, hereby revoking any and all Wills and Codicils heretofore made by me.

FIRST: I direct that all my just debts and funeral expenses be paid out of my estate as soon after my death as is practicable.

SECOND: I may leave a statement or list disposing of certain items of my tangible personal property. Any such statement or list in existence at the time of my death shall be determinative with respect to all items bequeathed therein.

THIRD: I give, devise, and bequeath all my estate, real, personal, and mixed, of whatever kind and wherever situated, of which I may die seized or possessed, or in which I may have any interest or over which I may have any power of appointment or testamentary disposition, as follows: _____% to my spouse, _____ and _____% to my children, _____ _____ _____,

in equal shares or to their lineal descendants per stirpes.

FOURTH: In the event that any beneficiary fails to survive me by thirty days, then this will shall take effect as if that person had predeceased me.

FIFTH: I hereby nominate, constitute, and appoint _____ as Personal Representative of this, my Last Will and Testament. In the event that such named person is unable or unwilling to serve at any time or for any reason, then I nominate, constitute, and appoint _____ as Personal Representative in the place and stead of the person first named herein. It is my will and I direct that my Personal Representative shall not be required to furnish a bond for the faithful performance of his or her duties in any jurisdiction, any provision of law to the contrary notwithstanding, and I give my Personal Representative full power to administer my estate, including the power to settle claims, pay debts, and sell, lease or exchange real and personal property without court order.

IN WITNESS WHEREOF I declare this to be my Last Will and Testament and execute it willingly as my free and voluntary act for the purposes expressed herein and I am of legal age and sound mind and make this under no constraint or undue influence, this _____ day of _____, _____ at _____ State of _____.

_____L.S.

The foregoing instrument was on said date subscribed at the end thereof by _____, the above named Testator who signed, published, and declared this instrument to be his/her Last Will and Testament in the presence of us and each of us, who thereupon at his/her request, in his/her presence, and in the presence of each other, have hereunto subscribed our names as witnesses thereto. We are of sound mind and proper age to witness a will and understand this to be his/her will, and to the best of our knowledge testator is of legal age to make a will, of sound mind, and under no constraint or undue influence.

_____residing at_____

_____residing at_____

Last Will and Testament

I, _____ a resident of _____ County, Florida do hereby make, publish, and declare this to be my Last Will and Testament, hereby revoking any and all Wills and Codicils heretofore made by me.

FIRST: I direct that all my just debts and funeral expenses be paid out of my estate as soon after my death as is practicable.

SECOND: I may leave a statement or list disposing of certain items of my tangible personal property. Any such statement or list in existence at the time of my death shall be determinative with respect to all items bequeathed therein.

THIRD: I give, devise, and bequeath all my estate, real, personal, and mixed, of whatever kind and wherever situated, of which I may die seized or possessed, or in which I may have any interest or over which I may have any power of appointment or testamentary disposition, to my children _____ _____ _____, plus any afterborn or adopted children in equal shares or to their lineal descendants per stirpes.

FOURTH: In the event that any beneficiary fails to survive me by thirty days, then this will shall take effect as if that person had predeceased me.

FIFTH: In the event any of my children have not attained the age of 18 years at the time of my death, I hereby nominate, constitute, and appoint _____ as guardian over the person and estate of any of my children who have not reached the age of majority at the time of my death. In the event that said guardian is unable or unwilling to serve, then I nominate, constitute, and appoint _____ as guardian. Said guardian shall serve without bond or surety.

SIXTH: I hereby nominate, constitute, and appoint _____ as Personal Representative of this, my Last Will and Testament. In the event that such named person is unable or unwilling to serve at any time or for any reason, then I nominate, constitute, and appoint _____ as Personal Representative in the place and stead of the person first named herein. It is my will and I direct that my Personal Representative shall not be required to furnish a bond for the faithful performance of his or her duties in any jurisdiction, any provision of law to the contrary notwithstanding, and I give my Personal Representative full power to administer my estate, including the power to settle claims, pay debts, and sell, lease or exchange real and personal property without court order.

IN WITNESS WHEREOF I declare this to be my Last Will and Testament and execute it willingly as my free and voluntary act for the purposes expressed herein and I am of legal age and sound mind and make this under no constraint or undue influence, this _____ day of _____, _____ at _____ State of _____.

_____L.S.

The foregoing instrument was on said date subscribed at the end thereof by _____, the above named Testator who signed, published, and declared this instrument to be his/her Last Will and Testament in the presence of us and each of us, who thereupon at his/her request, in his/her presence, and in the presence of each other, have hereunto subscribed our names as witnesses thereto. We are of sound mind and proper age to witness a will and understand this to be his/her will, and to the best of our knowledge testator is of legal age to make a will, of sound mind, and under no constraint or undue influence.

_____residing at_____

_____residing at_____

Last Will and Testament

I, _____ a resident of _____
County, Florida do hereby make, publish, and declare this to be my Last Will and Testament, hereby
revoking any and all Wills and Codicils heretofore made by me.

FIRST: I direct that all my just debts and funeral expenses be paid out of my estate as soon
after my death as is practicable.

SECOND: I may leave a statement or list disposing of certain items of my tangible personal
property. Any such statement or list in existence at the time of my death shall be determinative with
respect to all items bequeathed therein.

THIRD: I give, devise, and bequeath all my estate, real, personal, and mixed, of whatever
kind and wherever situated, of which I may die seized or possessed, or in which I may have any
interest or over which I may have any power of appointment or testamentary disposition, to my
children _____
_____
_____,
plus any afterborn or adopted children in equal shares or to their lineal descendants per stirpes.

FOURTH: In the event that any beneficiary fails to survive me by thirty days, then this will
shall take effect as if that person had predeceased me.

FIFTH: In the event any of my children have not attained the age of 18 years at the time of
my death, I hereby nominate, constitute, and appoint _____
as guardian over the person of any of my children who have not reached the age of majority at the
time of my death. In the event that said guardian is unable or unwilling to serve, then I nominate,
constitute, and appoint _____ as guardian. Said guardian
shall serve without bond or surety.

SIXTH: In the event any of my children have not attained the age of 18 years at the time of
my death, I hereby nominate, constitute, and appoint _____
as guardian over the estate of any of my children who have not reached the age of majority at the
time of my death. In the event that said guardian is unable or unwilling to serve, then I nominate,
constitute, and appoint _____ as guardian. Said guardian
shall serve without bond or surety.

SEVENTH: I hereby nominate, constitute, and appoint _____ as
Personal Representative of this, my Last Will and Testament. In the event that such named person
is unable or unwilling to serve at any time or for any reason, then I nominate, constitute, and appoint
_____ as Personal Representative in the place and stead of the per-
son first named herein. It is my will and I direct that my Personal Representative shall not be
required to furnish a bond for the faithful performance of his or her duties in any jurisdiction, any
provision of law to the contrary notwithstanding, and I give my Personal Representative full power

to administer my estate, including the power to settle claims, pay debts, and sell, lease or exchange real and personal property without court order.

IN WITNESS WHEREOF I declare this to be my Last Will and Testament and execute it willingly as my free and voluntary act for the purposes expressed herein and I am of legal age and sound mind and make this under no constraint or undue influence, this _____ day of _____, _____ at _____ State of _____.

_____L.S.

The foregoing instrument was on said date subscribed at the end thereof by _____, the above named Testator who signed, published, and declared this instrument to be his/her Last Will and Testament in the presence of us and each of us, who thereupon at his/her request, in his/her presence, and in the presence of each other, have hereunto subscribed our names as witnesses thereto. We are of sound mind and proper age to witness a will and understand this to be his/her will, and to the best of our knowledge testator is of legal age to make a will, of sound mind, and under no constraint or undue influence.

_____residing at_____

_____residing at_____

Last Will and Testament

I, _____ a resident of _____
County, Florida do hereby make, publish, and declare this to be my Last Will and Testament, hereby revoking any and all Wills and Codicils heretofore made by me.

FIRST: I direct that all my just debts and funeral expenses be paid out of my estate as soon after my death as is practicable.

SECOND: I may leave a statement or list disposing of certain items of my tangible personal property. Any such statement or list in existence at the time of my death shall be determinative with respect to all items bequeathed therein.

THIRD: I give, devise, and bequeath all my estate, real, personal, and mixed, of whatever kind and wherever situated, of which I may die seized or possessed, or in which I may have any interest or over which I may have any power of appointment or testamentary disposition, to my children _____
_____
_____,
plus any afterborn or adopted children in equal shares or to their lineal descendants per stirpes.

FOURTH: In the event that any beneficiary fails to survive me by thirty days, then this will shall take effect as if that person had predeceased me.

FIFTH: In the event that any of my children have not reached the age of _____ years at the time of my death, then the share of any such child shall be held in a separate trust by _____ for such child.

The trustee shall use the income and that part of the principal of the trust as is, in the trustee's sole discretion, necessary or desirable to provide proper housing, medical care, food, clothing, entertainment and education for the trust beneficiary, considering the beneficiary's other resources. Any income that is not distributed shall be added to the principal. Additionally, the trustee shall have all powers conferred by the law of the state having jurisdiction over this trust, as well as the power to pay from the assets of the trust reasonable fees necessary to administer the trust.

The trust shall terminate when the child reaches the age specified above and the remaining assets distributed to the child, unless they have been exhausted sooner. In the event the child dies prior to the termination of the trust, then the assets shall pass to the estate of the child. The interests of the beneficiary under this trust shall not be assignable and shall be free from the claims of creditors to the full extent allowed by law.

In the event the said trustee is unable or unwilling to serve for any reason, then I nominate, constitute, and appoint _____ as alternate trustee. No bond shall be required of either trustee in any jurisdiction and this trust shall be administered without court supervision as allowed by law.

SIXTH: In the event any of my children have not attained the age of 18 years at the time of my death, I hereby nominate, constitute, and appoint _____as guardian over the person and estate of any of my children who have not reached the age of majority at the time of my death. In the event that said guardian is unable or unwilling to serve, then I nominate, constitute, and appoint _____ as guardian. Said guardian shall serve without bond or surety.

SEVENTH: I hereby nominate, constitute, and appoint _____ as Personal Representative of this, my Last Will and Testament. In the event that such named person is unable or unwilling to serve at any time or for any reason, then I nominate, constitute, and appoint _____ as Personal Representative in the place and stead of the person first named herein. It is my will and I direct that my Personal Representative shall not be required to furnish a bond for the faithful performance of his or her duties in any jurisdiction, any provision of law to the contrary notwithstanding, and I give my Personal Representative full power to administer my estate, including the power to settle claims, pay debts, and sell, lease or exchange real and personal property without court order.

IN WITNESS WHEREOF I declare this to be my Last Will and Testament and execute it willingly as my free and voluntary act for the purposes expressed herein and I am of legal age and sound mind and make this under no constraint or undue influence, this _____ day of _____, _____ at _____ State of _____.

_____L.S.

The foregoing instrument was on said date subscribed at the end thereof by _____, the above named Testator who signed, published, and declared this instrument to be his/her Last Will and Testament in the presence of us and each of us, who thereupon at his/her request, in his/her presence, and in the presence of each other, have hereunto subscribed our names as witnesses thereto. We are of sound mind and proper age to witness a will and understand this to be his/her will, and to the best of our knowledge testator is of legal age to make a will, of sound mind, and under no constraint or undue influence.

_____residing at_____

_____residing at_____

Last Will and Testament

I, _____ a resident of _____ County, Florida do hereby make, publish, and declare this to be my Last Will and Testament, hereby revoking any and all Wills and Codicils heretofore made by me.

FIRST: I direct that all my just debts and funeral expenses be paid out of my estate as soon after my death as is practicable.

SECOND: I may leave a statement or list disposing of certain items of my tangible personal property. Any such statement or list in existence at the time of my death shall be determinative with respect to all items bequeathed therein.

THIRD: I give, devise, and bequeath all my estate, real, personal, and mixed, of whatever kind and wherever situated, of which I may die seized or possessed, or in which I may have any interest or over which I may have any power of appointment or testamentary disposition, to my children _____

_____

_____,

in equal shares, or their lineal descendants per stirpes.

FOURTH: In the event that any beneficiary fails to survive me by thirty days, then this will shall take effect as if that person had predeceased me.

FIFTH: I hereby nominate, constitute, and appoint _____ as Personal Representative of this, my Last Will and Testament. In the event that such named person is unable or unwilling to serve at any time or for any reason, then I nominate, constitute, and appoint _____ as Personal Representative in the place and stead of the person first named herein. It is my will and I direct that my Personal Representative shall not be required to furnish a bond for the faithful performance of his or her duties in any jurisdiction, any provision of law to the contrary notwithstanding, and I give my Personal Representative full power to administer my estate, including the power to settle claims, pay debts, and sell, lease or exchange real and personal property without court order.

IN WITNESS WHEREOF I declare this to be my Last Will and Testament and execute it willingly as my free and voluntary act for the purposes expressed herein and I am of legal age and sound mind and make this under no constraint or undue influence, this _____ day of _____, _____ at _____ State of _____.

_____ L.S.

The foregoing instrument was on said date subscribed at the end thereof by
_____, the above named Testator who signed, published,
and declared this instrument to be his/her Last Will and Testament in the presence of us and each of
us, who thereupon at his/her request, in his/her presence, and in the presence of each other, have
hereunto subscribed our names as witnesses thereto. We are of sound mind and proper age to witness a will and understand this to be his/her will, and to the best of our knowledge testator is of legal
age to make a will, of sound mind, and under no constraint or undue influence.

_____residing at_____

_____residing at_____

Last Will and Testament

I, _____ a resident of _____
County, Florida do hereby make, publish, and declare this to be my Last Will and Testament, hereby revoking any and all Wills and Codicils heretofore made by me.

FIRST: I direct that all my just debts and funeral expenses be paid out of my estate as soon after my death as is practicable.

SECOND: I may leave a statement or list disposing of certain items of my tangible personal property. Any such statement or list in existence at the time of my death shall be determinative with respect to all items bequeathed therein.

THIRD: I give, devise, and bequeath all my estate, real, personal, and mixed, of whatever kind and wherever situated, of which I may die seized or possessed, or in which I may have any interest or over which I may have any power of appointment or testamentary disposition, to my children _____

_____

_____,

in equal shares, or their lineal descendants per capita.

FOURTH: In the event that any beneficiary fails to survive me by thirty days, then this will shall take effect as if that person had predeceased me.

FIFTH: I hereby nominate, constitute, and appoint _____ as Personal Representative of this, my Last Will and Testament. In the event that such named person is unable or unwilling to serve at any time or for any reason, then I nominate, constitute, and appoint _____ as Personal Representative in the place and stead of the person first named herein. It is my will and I direct that my Personal Representative shall not be required to furnish a bond for the faithful performance of his or her duties in any jurisdiction, any provision of law to the contrary notwithstanding, and I give my Personal Representative full power to administer my estate, including the power to settle claims, pay debts, and sell, lease or exchange real and personal property without court order.

IN WITNESS WHEREOF I declare this to be my Last Will and Testament and execute it willingly as my free and voluntary act for the purposes expressed herein and I am of legal age and sound mind and make this under no constraint or undue influence, this _____ day of _____, _____ at _____ State of _____.

_____L.S.

The foregoing instrument was on said date subscribed at the end thereof by
_____, the above named Testator who signed, published, and declared this instrument to be his/her Last Will and Testament in the presence of us and each of us, who thereupon at his/her request, in his/her presence, and in the presence of each other, have hereunto subscribed our names as witnesses thereto. We are of sound mind and proper age to witness a will and understand this to be his/her will, and to the best of our knowledge testator is of legal age to make a will, of sound mind, and under no constraint or undue influence.

_____residing at_____

_____residing at_____

Last Will and Testament

I, _____ a resident of _____
County, Florida do hereby make, publish, and declare this to be my Last Will and Testament, hereby
revoking any and all Wills and Codicils heretofore made by me.

FIRST: I direct that all my just debts and funeral expenses be paid out of my estate as soon
after my death as is practicable.

SECOND: I may leave a statement or list disposing of certain items of my tangible personal
property. Any such statement or list in existence at the time of my death shall be determinative with
respect to all items bequeathed therein.

THIRD: I give, devise, and bequeath all my estate, real, personal, and mixed, of whatever
kind and wherever situated, of which I may die seized or possessed, or in which I may have any
interest or over which I may have any power of appointment or testamentary disposition, to the following: _____
_____
_____,

or to the survivor of them.

FOURTH: In the event that any beneficiary fails to survive me by thirty days, then this will
shall take effect as if that person had predeceased me.

FIFTH: I hereby nominate, constitute, and appoint _____ as
Personal Representative of this, my Last Will and Testament. In the event that such named person
is unable or unwilling to serve at any time or for any reason, then I nominate, constitute, and appoint
_____ as Personal Representative in the place and stead of the per-
son first named herein. It is my will and I direct that my Personal Representative shall not be
required to furnish a bond for the faithful performance of his or her duties in any jurisdiction, any
provision of law to the contrary notwithstanding, and I give my Personal Representative full power
to administer my estate, including the power to settle claims, pay debts, and sell, lease or exchange
real and personal property without court order.

IN WITNESS WHEREOF I declare this to be my Last Will and Testament and execute it
willingly as my free and voluntary act for the purposes expressed herein and I am of legal age and
sound mind and make this under no constraint or undue influence, this _____ day of
_____, _____ at _____ State of _____.

_____L.S.

The foregoing instrument was on said date subscribed at the end thereof by
_____, the above named Testator who signed, published, and declared this instrument to be his/her Last Will and Testament in the presence of us and each of us, who thereupon at his/her request, in his/her presence, and in the presence of each other, have hereunto subscribed our names as witnesses thereto. We are of sound mind and proper age to witness a will and understand this to be his/her will, and to the best of our knowledge testator is of legal age to make a will, of sound mind, and under no constraint or undue influence.

_____residing at_____

_____residing at_____

Last Will and Testament

I, _____ a resident of _____
County, Florida do hereby make, publish, and declare this to be my Last Will and Testament, hereby
revoking any and all Wills and Codicils heretofore made by me.

    FIRST: I direct that all my just debts and funeral expenses be paid out of my estate as soon
after my death as is practicable.

    SECOND: I may leave a statement or list disposing of certain items of my tangible personal
property. Any such statement or list in existence at the time of my death shall be determinative with
respect to all items bequeathed therein.

    THIRD: I give, devise, and bequeath all my estate, real, personal, and mixed, of whatever
kind and wherever situated, of which I may die seized or possessed, or in which I may have any
interest or over which I may have any power of appointment or testamentary disposition, to the following _____
_____
_____,

in equal shares, or their lineal descendants per stirpes.

    FOURTH: In the event that any beneficiary fails to survive me by thirty days, then this will
shall take effect as if that person had predeceased me.

    FIFTH: I hereby nominate, constitute, and appoint _____ as
Personal Representative of this, my Last Will and Testament. In the event that such named person
is unable or unwilling to serve at any time or for any reason, then I nominate, constitute, and appoint
_____ as Personal Representative in the place and stead of the per-
son first named herein. It is my will and I direct that my Personal Representative shall not be
required to furnish a bond for the faithful performance of his or her duties in any jurisdiction, any
provision of law to the contrary notwithstanding, and I give my Personal Representative full power
to administer my estate, including the power to settle claims, pay debts, and sell, lease or exchange
real and personal property without court order.

    IN WITNESS WHEREOF I declare this to be my Last Will and Testament and execute it
willingly as my free and voluntary act for the purposes expressed herein and I am of legal age and
sound mind and make this under no constraint or undue influence, this _____ day of
_____, _____ at _____ State of _____.

_____L.S.

The foregoing instrument was on said date subscribed at the end thereof by
_____, the above named Testator who signed, published, and declared this instrument to be his/her Last Will and Testament in the presence of us and each of us, who thereupon at his/her request, in his/her presence, and in the presence of each other, have hereunto subscribed our names as witnesses thereto. We are of sound mind and proper age to witness a will and understand this to be his/her will, and to the best of our knowledge testator is of legal age to make a will, of sound mind, and under no constraint or undue influence.

_____residing at_____

_____residing at_____

Self-Proved Will Affidavit
(attach to Will)

STATE OF FLORIDA

COUNTY OF _____

I,_____, declare to the officer taking my acknowledgment of this instrument, and to the subscribing witnesses, that I signed this instrument as my will.

_____
Testator

We, _____ and _____, have been sworn by the officer signing below, and declare to that officer on our oaths that the testator declared the instrument to be the testator's will and signed it in our presence and that we each signed the instrument as a witness in the presence of the testator and of each other.

_____
Witness

_____
Witness

Acknowledged and subscribed before me by the testator, _____ who is personally known to me or who has produced _____ as identification, and sworn to and subscribed before me by the witnesses, _____ who is personally known to me or who has produced _____ as identification and _____ who is personally known to me or who has produced _____ as identification, and subscribed by me in the presence of the testator and the subscribing witnesses, all on _____, 20___.

_____
Notary or other officer

This page intentionally blank.

Codicil to the Will of

_____

I, _____, a resident of _____
County, Florida declare this to be the first codicil to my Last Will and Testament dated
_____, _____.

FIRST: I hereby revoke the clause of my Will which reads as follows:_____
_____
_____
_____
_____.

SECOND: I hereby add the following clause to my Will: _____
_____
_____
_____.

THIRD: In all other respects I hereby confirm and republish my Last Will and Testament
dated _____, _____.

IN WITNESS WHEREOF, I have signed, published, and declared the foregoing instrument
as and for a codicil to my Last Will and Testament, this _____ day of
_____, _____.

_____

The foregoing instrument was on the _____day of _____, _____,
signed at the end thereof, and at the same time published and declared by
_____, as and for a codicil to his/her Last Will and Testament,
dated _____, _____, in the presence of each of us, who, this attestation
clause having been read to us, did at the request of the said testator/testatrix, in his/her presence and
in the presence of each other signed our names as witnesses thereto.

_____residing at_____

_____residing at_____

This page intentionally blank.

Self-Proved Codicil Affidavit

(attach to Codicil)

STATE OF FLORIDA

COUNTY OF _____

I, _____, declare to the officer taking my acknowledgment of this instrument, and to the subscribing witnesses, that I signed this instrument as my will.

_____
Testator

We, _____ and _____, have been sworn by the officer signing below, and declare to that officer on our oaths that the testator declared the instrument to be the testator's will and signed it in our presence and that we each signed the instrument as a witness in the presence of the testator and of each other.

_____
Witness

_____
Witness

Acknowledged and subscribed before me by the testator, _____ who is personally known to me or who has produced _____ as identification, and sworn to and subscribed before me by the witnesses, _____ who is personally known to me or who has produced _____ as identification and _____ who is personally known to me or who has produced _____ as identification, and subscribed by me in the presence of the testator and the subscribing witnesses, all on _____, 20___.

_____
Notary or other officer

This page intentionally blank.

Living Will

Declaration made this _____ day of _____, 20_____. I, _____, willfully and voluntarily make known my desire that my dying not be artificially prolonged under the circumstances set forth below, and I do hereby declare that, if at any time I am both mentally and physically incapacitated

_____ and I have a terminal condition

or _____ and I have an end-state condition

or _____ and I am in a persistent vegetative state

and if my attending or treating physician and another consulting physician have determined that there is no reasonable medical probability of my recovery from such condition, I direct that life-pro-longing procedures be withheld or withdrawn when the application of such procedures would serve only to prolong artificially the process of dying, and that I be permitted to die naturally with only the administration of medication or the performance of any medical procedure deemed necessary to provide me with comfort care or to alleviate pain.

It is my intention that this declaration be honored by my family and physician as the final expression of my legal right to refuse medical or surgical treatment and to accept the consequences for such refusal.

In the event that I have been determined to be unable to provide express and informed con-sent regarding the withholding, withdrawal, or continuation of life-prolonging procedures, I wish to designate, as my surrogate to carry out the provisions of this declaration:

Name:_____

Address:_____

_____ Zip Code:_____

Phone: _____

I understand the full import of this declaration, and am emotionally and mentally competent to make this declaration.

Additional instructions (optional):

_____

_____

_____

(Signed)

_____   _____

Witness   Witness

_____   _____

_____   _____

Address   Address

_____   _____

Phone   Phone

This page intentionally blank.

UNIFORM DONOR CARD

The undersigned hereby makes this anatomical gift, if medically acceptable, to take effect on death. The words and marks below indicate my desires:

I give:

        (a) _____ any needed organs or parts;

        (b) _____ only the following organs or parts

_____

for the purpose of transplantation, therapy, medical research, or education;

        (c) _____ my body for anatomical study if needed.

Limitations or special wishes, if any:

_____

Signed by the donor and the following witnesses in the presence of each other:

_____   _____
Signature of Donor   Date of birth

_____   _____
Date signed   City & State

_____   _____
Witness   Witness

_____   _____
Address   Address

UNIFORM DONOR CARD

The undersigned hereby makes this anatomical gift, if medically acceptable, to take effect on death. The words and marks below indicate my desires:

I give:

        (a) _____ any needed organs or parts;

        (b) _____ only the following organs or parts

_____

for the purpose of transplantation, therapy, medical research, or education;

        (c) _____ my body for anatomical study if needed.

Limitations or special wishes, if any:

_____

Signed by the donor and the following witnesses in the presence of each other:

_____   _____
Signature of Donor   Date of birth

_____   _____
Date signed   City & State

_____   _____
Witness   Witness

_____   _____
Address   Address

UNIFORM DONOR CARD

The undersigned hereby makes this anatomical gift, if medically acceptable, to take effect on death. The words and marks below indicate my desires:

I give:

        (a) _____ any needed organs or parts;

        (b) _____ only the following organs or parts

_____

for the purpose of transplantation, therapy, medical research, or education;

        (c) _____ my body for anatomical study if needed.

Limitations or special wishes, if any:

_____

Signed by the donor and the following witnesses in the presence of each other:

_____   _____
Signature of Donor   Date of birth

_____   _____
Date signed   City & State

_____   _____
Witness   Witness

_____   _____
Address   Address

UNIFORM DONOR CARD

The undersigned hereby makes this anatomical gift, if medically acceptable, to take effect on death. The words and marks below indicate my desires:

I give:

        (a) _____ any needed organs or parts;

        (b) _____ only the following organs or parts

_____

for the purpose of transplantation, therapy, medical research, or education;

        (c) _____ my body for anatomical study if needed.

Limitations or special wishes, if any:

_____

Signed by the donor and the following witnesses in the presence of each other:

_____   _____
Signature of Donor   Date of birth

_____   _____
Date signed   City & State

_____   _____
Witness   Witness

_____   _____
Address   Address

One of these cards should be cut out and carried in your wallet or purse.

INDEX

Your #1 Source for Real World Legal Information...

SPHINX® PUBLISHING
An Imprint of Sourcebooks, Inc.®

- Written by lawyers
- Simple English explanation of the law
- Forms and instructions included

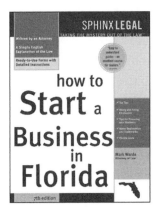

How to Start a Business in Florida, 7E

The essential book for starting a business in Florida, this title explains all the steps necessary in clear language. Includes blank form and detailed instructions for completing them.

280 pages; $21.95;
ISBN 1-57248-339-3

How to File for Divorce in Florida, 8E

This all-inclusive manual contains valuable explanation of child custody, visitation, alimony and many other legal topics. Includes ready-to-use forms

376 pages; $28.95;
ISBN 1-57248-396-2

Landlords' Rights & Duties in Florida, 9E

A concise guide that covers every legal topic concerning a landlord. Includes valuable Florida forms as well as numerous other resources.

256 pages; $22.95;
ISBN 1-57248-338-5

See the following order form for books written specifically for California,
the District of Columbia, Florida, Georgia, Illinois, Maryland, Massachusetts, Michigan,
Minnesota, New Jersey, New York, North Carolina,
Ohio, Pennsylvania, Texas, and Virginia!

What our customers say about our books:

"It couldn't be more clear for the lay person." —R.D.

"I want you to know I really appreciate your book. It has saved me a lot of time and money." —L.T.

"Your real estate contracts book has saved me nearly $12,000.00 in closing costs over the past year." —A.B.

"...many of the legal questions that I have had over the years were answered clearly and concisely through your plain English interpretation of the law." —C.E.H.

"If there weren't people out there like you I'd be lost. You have the best books of this type out there." —S.B.

"...your forms and directions are easy to follow." —C.V.M.

SPHINX® PUBLISHING'S STATE TITLES
Up-to-Date for Your State

California Titles

CA Power of Attorney Handbook (2E)	$18.95
How to File for Divorce in CA (4E)	$26.95
How to Settle & Probate an Estate in CA (2E)	$28.95
How to Start a Business in CA (2E)	$21.95
How to Win in Small Claims Court in CA (2E)	$18.95
The Landlord's Legal Guide in CA (2E)	$24.95
Make Your Own CA Will	$18.95
Tenants' Rights in CA	$21.95

Florida Titles

Child Custody, Visitation and Support in FL	$26.95
How to File for Divorce in FL (8E)	$28.95
How to Form a Corporation in FL (6E)	$24.95
How to Form a Limited Liability Co. in FL (2E)	$24.95
How to Form a Partnership in FL	$22.95
How to Make a FL Will (7E)	$16.95
How to Probate and Settle an Estate in FL (5E)	$26.95
How to Start a Business in FL (7E)	$21.95
How to Win in Small Claims Court in FL (7E)	$18.95
Land Trusts in Florida (6E)	$29.95
Landlords' Rights and Duties in FL (9E)	$22.95

Georgia Titles

How to File for Divorce in GA (5E)	$21.95
How to Make a GA Will (4E)	$16.95
How to Start a Business in Georgia (3E)	$21.95

Illinois Titles

Child Custody, Visitation and Support in IL	$24.95
How to File for Divorce in IL (3E)	$24.95
How to Make an IL Will (3E)	$16.95
How to Start a Business in IL (4E)	$21.95
The Landlord's Legal Guide in IL	$24.95

Maryland, Virginia and the District of Columbia Titles

How to File for Divorce in MD, VA and DC	$28.95
How to Start a Business in MD, VA or DC	$21.95

Massachusetts Titles

How to Form a Corporation in MA	$24.95
How to Make a MA Will (2E)	$16.95
How to Start a Business in MA (4E)	$21.95
The Landlord's Legal Guide in MA (2E)	$24.95

Michigan Titles

How to File for Divorce in MI (3E)	$24.95
How to Make a MI Will (3E)	$16.95
How to Start a Business in MI (4E)	$24.95

Minnesota Titles

How to File for Divorce in MN	$21.95
How to Form a Corporation in MN	$24.95
How to Make a MN Will (2E)	$16.95

New Jersey Titles

How to File for Divorce in NJ	$24.95
How to Start a Business in NJ	$21.95

New York Titles

Child Custody, Visitation and Support in NY	$26.95
File for Divorce in NY	$26.95
How to Form a Corporation in NY (2E)	$24.95
How to Make a NY Will (3E)	$16.95
How to Start a Business in NY (2E)	$18.95
How to Win in Small Claims Court in NY (2E)	$18.95
Landlords' Legal Guide in NY	$24.95
New York Power of Attorney Handbook	$19.95
Tenants' Rights in NY	$21.95

North Carolina and South Carolina Titles

How to File for Divorce in NC (3E)	$22.95
How to Make a NC Will (3E)	$16.95
How to Start a Business in NC or SC	$24.95
Landlords' Rights & Duties in NC	$21.95

Ohio Titles

How to File for Divorce in OH (2E)	$24.95
How to Form a Corporation in OH	$24.95
How to Make an OH Will	$16.95

Pennsylvania Titles

Child Custody, Visitation and Support in PA	$26.95
How to File for Divorce in PA (3E)	$26.95
How to Form a Corporation in PA	$24.95
How to Make a PA Will (2E)	$16.95
How to Start a Business in PA (3E)	$21.95
The Landlord's Legal Guide in PA	$24.95

Texas Titles

Child Custody, Visitation and Support in TX	$22.95
How to File for Divorce in TX (4E)	$24.95
How to Form a Corporation in TX (3E)	$24.95
How to Make a TX Will (3E)	$16.95
How to Probate and Settle an Estate in TX (3E)	$26.95
How to Start a Business in TX (4E)	$21.95
How to Win in Small Claims Court in TX (2E)	$16.95
The Landlord's Legal Guide in TX	$24.95

Sphinx® Publishing's National Titles
Valid in All 50 States

LEGAL SURVIVAL IN BUSINESS

The Complete Book of Corporate Forms	$24.95
The Complete Partnership Book	$24.95
The Complete Patent Book	$26.95
Employees' Rights	$18.95
Employer's Rights	$24.95
The Entrepreneur's Internet Handbook	$21.95
The Entrepreneur's Legal Guide	$26.95
Financing Your Small Business	$17.95
How to Buy a Franchise	$19.95
How to Form a Limited Liability Company (2E)	$24.95
How to Form a Nonprofit Corporation (3E)	$24.95
How to Form Your Own Corporation (4E)	$26.95
How to Register Your Own Copyright (5E)	$24.95
How to Register Your Own Trademark (3E)	$21.95
Incorporate in Delaware from Any State	$26.95
Incorporate in Nevada from Any State	$24.95
The Law (In Plain English)® for Small Business	$19.95
Most Valuable Business Legal Forms You'll Ever Need (3E)	$21.95
Profit from Intellectual Property	$28.95
Protect Your Patent	$24.95
The Small Business Owner's Guide to Bankruptcy	$21.95
Tax Smarts for Small Business	$21.95

LEGAL SURVIVAL IN COURT

Attorney Responsibilities & Client Rights	$19.95
Crime Victim's Guide to Justice (2E)	$21.95
Help Your Lawyer Win Your Case (2E)	$14.95
Legal Research Made Easy (3E)	$21.95
Winning Your Personal Injury Claim (2E)	$24.95

LEGAL SURVIVAL IN REAL ESTATE

The Complete Kit to Selling Your Own Home	$18.95
Essential Guide to Real Estate Contracts (2E)	$18.95
Essential Guide to Real Estate Leases	$18.95
Homeowner's Rights	$19.95
How to Buy a Condominium or Townhome (2E)	$19.95
How to Buy Your First Home	$18.95
Working with Your Homeowners Association	$19.95

LEGAL SURVIVAL IN SPANISH

Cómo Hacer su Propio Testamento	$16.95
Cómo Restablecer su propio Crédito y Renegociar sus Deudas	$21.95
Cómo Solicitar su Propio Divorcio	$24.95
Guía de Inmigración a Estados Unidos (4E)	$24.95
Guía de Justicia para Víctimas del Crimen	$21.95
Guía Esencial para los Contratos de Arrendamiento de Bienes Raices	$22.95
Inmigración y Ciudadanía en los EE. UU. Preguntas y Respuestas	$16.95
Inmigración a los EE. UU. Paso a Paso (2E)	$24.95
Manual de Beneficios para el Seguro Social	$18.95
El Seguro Social Preguntas y Respuestas	$16.95

LEGAL SURVIVAL IN PERSONAL AFFAIRS

101 Complaint Letters That Get Results	$18.95
The 529 College Savings Plan (2E)	$18.95
The Antique and Art Collector's Legal Guide	$24.95
Child Support	$18.95
The Complete Adoption and Fertility Legal Guide	$24.95
The Complete Book of Insurance	$18.95
The Complete Legal Guide to Senior Care	$21.95
Credit Smart	$18.95
Fathers' Rights	$19.95
Family Limited Partnership	$26.95
Gay & Lesbian Rights	$26.95
Grandparents' Rights (3E)	$24.95
How to File Your Own Bankruptcy (5E)	$21.95
How to File Your Own Divorce (5E)	$26.95
How to Make Your Own Simple Will (3E)	$18.95
How to Write Your Own Living Will (4E)	$18.95
How to Write Your Own Premarital Agreement (3E)	$24.95
Law School 101	$16.95
The Living Trust Kit	$21.95
Living Trusts and Other Ways to Avoid Probate (3E)	$24.95
Mastering the MBE	$16.95
Most Valuable Personal Legal Forms You'll Ever Need (2E)	$26.95
Nursing Homes and Assisted Living Facilities	$19.95
The Power of Attorney Handbook (5E)	$22.95
Repair Your Own Credit and Deal with Debt (2E)	$18.95
Quick Cash	$14.95
Sexual Harassment:Your Guide to Legal Action	$18.95
Seniors' Rights	$19.95
Sisters-in-Law	$16.95
The Social Security Benefits Handbook (4E)	$18.95
Social Security Q&A	$12.95
Starting Our or Starting Over	$14.95
Teen Rights	$22.95
Traveler's Rights	$21.95
Unmarried Parents' Rights (2E)	$19.95
U.S. Immigration and Citizenship Q&A	$18.95
U.S. Immigration Step by Step (2E)	$24.95
U.S.A. Immigration Guide (5E)	$26.95
The Visitation Handbook	$18.95
The Wills, Estate Planning and Trusts Legal Kit	&26.95
Win Your Unemployment Compensation Claim (2E)	$21.95
Your Right to Child Custody, Visitation and Support (3E)	$24.95

SPHINX® PUBLISHING ORDER FORM

BILL TO:		SHIP TO:	
Phone #	Terms	F.O.B. Chicago, IL	Ship Date

Charge my: ☐ VISA ☐ MasterCard ☐ American Express

☐ **Money Order or Personal Check**

Credit Card Number

Expiration Date

Qty	ISBN	Title	Retail	Ext.	Qty	ISBN	Title	Retail	Ext.
		SPHINX PUBLISHING NATIONAL TITLES				1-57248-156-0	How to Write Your Own Premarital Agreement (3E)	$24.95	
	1-57248-363-6	101 Complaint Letters That Get Results	$18.95			1-57248-230-3	Incorporate in Delaware from Any State	$26.95	
	1-57248-361-X	The 529 College Savings Plan (2E)	$18.95			1-57248-158-7	Incorporate in Nevada from Any State	$24.95	
	1-57248-349-0	The Antique and Art Collector's Legal Guide	$24.95			1-57248-474-8	Inmigración a los EE.UU. Paso a Paso (2E)	$24.95	
	1-57248-347-4	Attorney Responsibilities & Client Rights	$19.95			1-57248-400-4	Inmigración y Ciudadanía en los EE.UU. Preguntas y Respuestas	$16.95	
	1-57248-382-2	Child Support	$18.95			1-57248-374-1	Law School 101	$16.95	
	1-57248-148-X	Cómo Hacer su Propio Testamento	$16.95			1-57248-377-6	The Law (In Plain English)® for Small Business	$19.95	
	1-57248-226-5	Cómo Restablecer su propio Crédito y Renegociar sus Deudas	$21.95			1-57248-223-0	Legal Research Made Easy (3E)	$21.95	
	1-57248-147-1	Cómo Solicitar su Propio Divorcio	$24.95			1-57248-449-7	The Living Trust Kit	$21.95	
	1-57248-373-3	`The Complete Adoption and Fertility Legal Guide	$24.95			1-57248-165-X	Living Trusts and Other Ways to Avoid Probate (3E)	$24.95	
	1-57248-166-8	The Complete Book of Corporate Forms	$24.95			1-57248-186-2	Manual de Beneficios para el Seguro Social	$18.95	
	1-57248-383-0	The Complete Book of Insurance	$18.95			1-57248-220-6	Mastering the MBE	$16.95	
	1-57248-353-9	The Complete Kit to Selling Your Own Home	$18.95			1-57248-167-6	Most Val. Business Legal Forms You'll Ever Need (3E)	$21.95	
	1-57248-229-X	The Complete Legal Guide to Senior Care	$21.95			1-57248-360-1	Most Val. Personal Legal Forms You'll Ever Need (2E)	$26.95	
	1-57248-391-1	The Complete Partnership Book	$24.95			1-57248-388-1	The Power of Attorney Handbook (5E)	$22.95	
	1-57248-201-X	The Complete Patent Book	$26.95			1-57248-332-6	Profit from Intellectual Property	$28.95	
	1-57248-369-5	Credit Smart	$18.95			1-57248-329-6	Protect Your Patent	$24.95	
	1-57248-163-3	Crime Victim's Guide to Justice (2E)	$21.95			1-57248-376-8	Nursing Homes and Assisted Living Facilities	$19.95	
	1-57248-367-9	Employees' Rights	$18.95			1-57248-385-7	Quick Cash	$14.95	
	1-57248-365-2	Employer's Rights	$24.95			1-57248-344-X	Repair Your Own Credit and Deal with Debt (2E)	$18.95	
	1-57248-251-6	The Entrepreneur's Internet Handbook	$21.95			1-57248-350-4	El Seguro Social Preguntas y Respuestas	$16.95	
	1-57248-235-4	The Entrepreneur's Legal Guide	$26.95			1-57248386-5	Seniors' Rights	$19.95	
	1-57248-346-6	Essential Guide to Real Estate Contracts (2E)	$18.95			1-57248-217-6	Sexual Harassment: Your Guide to Legal Action	$18.95	
	1-57248-160-9	Essential Guide to Real Estate Leases	$18.95			1-57248-378-4	Sisters-in-Law	$16.95	
	1-57248-254-0	Family Limited Partnership	$26.95			1-57248-219-2	The Small Business Owner's Guide to Bankruptcy	$21.95	
	1-57248-375-X	Fathers' Rights	$19.95			1-57248-395-4	The Social Security Benefits Handbook (4E)	$18.95	
	1-57248-450-0	Financing Your Small Business	$17.95			1-57248-216-8	Social Security Q&A	$12.95	
	1-57248-331-8	Gay & Lesbian Rights	$26.95			1-57248-328-8	Starting Out or Starting Over	$14.95	
	1-57248-139-0	Grandparents' Rights (3E)	$24.95			1-57248-221-4	Teen Rights	$22.95	
	1-57248-475-6	Guía de Inmigración a Estados Unidos (4E)	$24.95			1-57248-366-0	Tax Smarts for Small Business	$21.95	
	1-57248-187-0	Guía de Justicia para Víctimas del Crimen	$21.95			1-57248-335-0	Traveler's Rights	$21.95	
	1-57248-253-2	Guía Esencial para los Contratos de Arrendamiento de Bienes Raices	$22.95			1-57248-236-2	Unmarried Parents' Rights (2E)	$19.95	
	1-57248-103-X	Help Your Lawyer Win Your Case (2E)	$14.95			1-57248-362-8	U.S. Immigration and Citizenship Q&A	$18.95	
	1-57248-334-2	Homeowner's Rights	$19.95			1-57248-387-3	U.S. Immigration Step by Step (2E)	$24.95	
	1-57248-164-1	How to Buy a Condominium or Townhome (2E)	$19.95			1-57248-392-X	U.S.A. Immigration Guide (5E)	$26.95	
	1-57248-328-8	How to Buy Your First Home	$18.95			1-57248-192-7	The Visitation Handbook	$18.95	
	1-57248-384-9	How to Buy a Franchise	$19.95			1-57248-225-7	Win Your Unemployment Compensation Claim (2E)	$21.95	
	1-57248-191-9	How to File Your Own Bankruptcy (5E)	$21.95			1-57248-330-X	The Wills, Estate Planning and Trusts Legal Kit	&26.95	
	1-57248-343-1	How to File Your Own Divorce (5E)	$26.95			1-57248-138-2	Winning Your Personal Injury Claim (2E)	$24.95	
	1-57248-222-2	How to Form a Limited Liability Company (2E)	$24.95			1-57248-333-4	Working with Your Homeowners Association	$19.95	
	1-57248-390-3	How to Form a Nonprofit Corporation (3E)	$24.95			1-57248-380-6	Your Right to Child Custody, Visitation and Support (3E)	$24.95	
	1-57248-345-8	How to Form Your Own Corporation (4E)	$26.95						
	1-57248-232-X	How to Make Your Own Simple Will (3E)	$18.95						
	1-57248-379-2	How to Register Your Own Copyright (5E)	$24.95						
	1-57248-104-8	How to Register Your Own Trademark (3E)	$21.95						
	1-57248-394-6	How to Write Your Own Living Will (4E)	$18.95						

Form Continued on Following Page   **SubTotal** _____

To order, call Sourcebooks at 1-800-432-7444 or FAX (630) 961-2168 (Bookstores, libraries, wholesalers—please call for discount)

Prices are subject to change without notice.

Find more legal information at: **www.SphinxLegal.com**

SPHINX® PUBLISHING ORDER FORM

Qty	ISBN	Title	Retail	Ext.
		CALIFORNIA TITLES		
___	1-57248-150-1	CA Power of Attorney Handbook (2E)	$18.95	___
___	1-57248-337-7	How to File for Divorce in CA (4E)	$26.95	___
___	1-57248-464-0	How to Settle and Probate an Estate in CA	$28.95	___
___	1-57248-336-9	How to Start a Business in CA (2E)	$21.95	___
___	1-57248-194-3	How to Win in Small Claims Court in CA (2E)	$18.95	___
___	1-57248-246-X	Make Your Own CA Will	$18.95	___
___	1-57248-397-0	The Landlord's Legal Guide in CA (2E)	$24.95	___
___	1-57248-241-9	Tenants' Rights in CA	$21.95	___
		FLORIDA TITLES		
___	1-57071-363-4	Florida Power of Attorney Handbook (2E)	$16.95	___
___	1-57248-396-2	How to File for Divorce in FL (8E)	$28.95	___
___	1-57248-356-3	How to Form a Corporation in FL (6E)	$24.95	___
___	1-57248-203-6	How to Form a Limited Liability Co. in FL (2E)	$24.95	___
___	1-57071-401-0	How to Form a Partnership in FL	$22.95	___
___	1-57248-456-X	How to Make a FL Will (7E)	$16.95	___
___	1-57248-088-2	How to Modify Your FL Divorce Judgment (4E)	$24.95	___
___	1-57248-354-7	How to Probate and Settle an Estate in FL (5E)	$26.95	___
___	1-57248-339-3	How to Start a Business in FL (7E)	$21.95	___
___	1-57248-204-4	How to Win in Small Claims Court in FL (7E)	$18.95	___
___	1-57248-381-4	Land Trusts in Florida (7E)	$29.95	___
___	1-57248-338-5	Landlords' Rights and Duties in FL (9E)	$22.95	___
		GEORGIA TITLES		
___	1-57248-340-7	How to File for Divorce in GA (5E)	$21.95	___
___	1-57248-180-3	How to Make a GA Will (4E)	$16.95	___
___	1-57248-341-5	How to Start a Business in Georgia (3E)	$21.95	___
		ILLINOIS TITLES		
___	1-57248-244-3	Child Custody, Visitation, and Support in IL	$24.95	___
___	1-57248-206-0	How to File for Divorce in IL (3E)	$24.95	___
___	1-57248-170-6	How to Make an IL Will (3E)	$16.95	___
___	1-57248-265-9	How to Start a Business in IL (4E)	$21.95	___
___	1-57248-252-4	The Landlord's Legal Guide in IL	$24.95	___
		MARYLAND, VIRGINIA AND THE DISTRICT OF COLUMBIA		
___	1-57248-240-0	How to File for Divorce in MD, VA and DC	$28.95	___
___	1-57248-359-8	How to Start a Business in MD, VA or DC	$21.95	___
		MASSACHUSETTS TITLES		
___	1-57248-128-5	How to File for Divorce in MA (3E)	$24.95	___
___	1-57248-115-3	How to Form a Corporation in MA	$24.95	___
___	1-57248-108-0	How to Make a MA Will (2E)	$16.95	___
___	1-57248-466-7	How to Start a Business in MA (4E)	$21.95	___
___	1-57248-398-9	The Landlord's Legal Guide in MA (2E)	$24.95	___
		MICHIGAN TITLES		
___	1-57248-215-X	How to File for Divorce in MI (3E)	$24.95	___
___	1-57248-182-X	How to Make a MI Will (3E)	$16.95	___
___	1-57248-183-8	How to Start a Business in MI (3E)	$18.95	___
		MINNESOTA TITLES		
___	1-57248-142-0	How to File for Divorce in MN	$21.95	___
___	1-57248-179-X	How to Form a Corporation in MN	$24.95	___
___	1-57248-178-1	How to Make a MN Will (2E)	$16.95	___
		NEW JERSEY TITLES		
___	1-57248-239-7	How to File for Divorce in NJ	$24.95	___
___	1-57248-448-9	How to Start a Business in NJ	$21.95	___

Qty	ISBN	Title	Retail	Ext.
		NEW YORK TITLES		
___	1-57248-193-5	Child Custody, Visitation and Support in NY	$26.95	___
___	1-57248-351-2	File for Divorce in NY	$26.95	___
___	1-57248-249-4	How to Form a Corporation in NY (2E)	$24.95	___
___	1-57248-401-2	How to Make a NY Will (3E)	$16.95	___
___	1-57248-199-4	How to Start a Business in NY (2E)	$18.95	___
___	1-57248-198-6	How to Win in Small Claims Court in NY (2E)	$18.95	___
___	1-57248-197-8	Landlords' Legal Guide in NY	$24.95	___
___	1-57071-188-7	New York Power of Attorney Handbook	$19.95	___
___	1-57248-122-6	Tenants' Rights in NY	$21.95	___
		NORTH CAROLINA TITLES		
___	1-57248-185-4	How to File for Divorce in NC (3E)	$22.95	___
___	1-57248-129-3	How to Make a NC Will (3E)	$16.95	___
___	1-57248-184-6	How to Start a Business in NC (3E)	$18.95	___
___	1-57248-091-2	Landlords' Rights & Duties in NC	$21.95	___
		NORTH CAROLINA AND SOUTH CAROLINA TITLES		
___	1-57248-371-7	How to Start a Business in NC or SC	$24.95	___
		OHIO TITLES		
___	1-57248-190-0	How to File for Divorce in OH (2E)	$24.95	___
___	1-57248-174-9	How to Form a Corporation in OH	$24.95	___
___	1-57248-173-0	How to Make an OH Will	$16.95	___
		PENNSYLVANIA TITLES		
___	1-57248-242-7	Child Custody, Visitation and Support in PA	$26.95	___
___	1-57248-211-7	How to File for Divorce in PA (3E)	$26.95	___
___	1-57248-358-X	How to Form a Cooporation in PA	$24.95	___
___	1-57248-094-7	How to Make a PA Will (2E)	$16.95	___
___	1-57248-357-1	How to Start a Business in PA (3E)	$21.95	___
___	1-57248-245-1	The Landlord's Legal Guide in PA	$24.95	___
		TEXAS TITLES		
___	1-57248-171-4	Child Custody, Visitation, and Support in TX	$22.95	___
___	1-57248-399-7	How to File for Divorce in TX (4E)	$24.95	___
___	1-57248-470-5	How to Form a Corporation in TX (3E)	$24.95	___
___	1-57248-255-9	How to Make a TX Will (3E)	$16.95	___
___	1-57248-214-1	How to Probate and Settle an Estate in TX (3E)	$26.95	___
___	1-57248-471-3	How to Start a Business in TX (4E)	$21.95	___
___	1-57248-111-0	How to Win in Small Claims Court in TX (2E)	$16.95	___
___	1-57248-355-5	The Landlord's Legal Guide in TX	$24.95	___

SubTotal This page   ___

SubTotal previous page   ___

Shipping — $5.00 for 1st book, $1.00 each additional ___

Illinois residents add 6.75% sales tax ___

Connecticut residents add 6.00% sales tax ___

Total   ___

To order, call Sourcebooks at 1-800-432-7444 or FAX (630) 961-2168 (Bookstores, libraries, wholesalers—please call for discount)

Prices are subject to change without notice.

Find more legal information at: **www.SphinxLegal.com**